Large Print Edition

Rebel Canners Cookbook

Preserving Time-Honored Methods

By Tammy McNeill

Copyright © 2018 by Tammy McNeil

All rights reserved. Printed in the United States of America. No part of this book may be used or reproduced in any manner whatsoever without written permission except in the case of brief quotations embodied in critical articles and reviews.

For more information please contact Tammy McNeill at:
rebelcanners@gmail.com

ISBN 978-1-7327514-4-6 Large Print Hardback 8.5x11

Contents

Dedication 5
Special Thanks 9

I. CONDIMENTS 12

01. Baby Sauce 12
02. Bread and Butter Fiddleheads 13
03. Bread and Butter Pickles 16
04. Brown Sugar Sauce 18
05. Black Bean Dip 19
06. Cowboy Candy 22
07. Cranberry Ketchup 23
08. Cranberry Relish 27
09. Fireweed Honey 30
10. Flavored Extracts 34
11. Lard, Butter, Bacon 35
12. Margarine 38
13. Pineapple Topping 39
14. Rose Water Syrup 42
15. Refrigerator Pickles 43
16. Sweet Relish 46

II. BREADS 50

17. Baked Pancake 50
18. French Toast 51
19. Tortillas (Flour) 52

III. DESSERTS 53

20. Chocolate Pie (Christmas) 53
21. Christmas Finger Jell-O 56
22. Rum Cake 57
23. Strawberry Rhubarb Pie Filling 60
24. Thumbprint Cookies 61
25. Zucchini Cookies 64

IV. FRUITS 65

26. Cranberry Juice 65
27. Pumpkin (Cubed) 68
28. Pumpkin Seeds 69
29. Rhubarb Fruit Leather 72

V. JELLY, JAM & BUTTERS 73

30. Apple Butter 73
31. Pumpkin Butter 76
32. Strawberry Jam 77
33. Tipsy Peach Jam 80
34. Cherry Jam 81
35. Apple Cider Jelly 82
36. Elderberry Jelly 83
37. Apple Jelly (without added pectin) 86
38. Dandelion Jelly 87
39. Elderberry Juice 90
40. Elderberry Syrup (Basic) 91
41. Wild Violet Jelly 94

VI. MEATS 95

42. Hot Dogs — 95
43. Chicken Bone Broth — 98
44. Chicken and Dumplings — 99
45. Chicken Soup Starter — 102
46. Corned Beef Hash — 103
47. Corned Venison — 104
48. Ham and Cheese Ball (Christmas) — 105
49. Ham (Deviled) — 108
50. Ham Loaf — 109
51. Ham (Omelette) — 112
52. Pork Roast — 113
53. Sweet and Sour Chicken — 116
54. Laura's Egg Rolls — 117
55. Taco Seasoning and Taco Meat — 120

VII. MILK PRODUCTS — 121

56. Cheese Sauce — 121
57. Cream Cheese — 124
58. Crockpot Yogurt — 125
59. Milk — 128
60. Shepherd Maple Butter — 129

VIII. PASTA & NOODLES — 132

61. Grandma's Noodles — 132
62. Macaroni and Tomatoes — 133
63. Tortellini In Marinara Sauce — 136

IX. SALADS — 137

64. Cucumber And Onion Salad — 137
65. Slaw — 140

X. VEGGIES — 141

66. Beans — 141
67. Bean Soup (Grandma's) — 144
68. Cauliflower (Pickled) — 145
69. Corn Casserole (Thanksgiving) — 148
70. Giardiniera (Overnight, Refrigerated) — 149
71. Peppers In A Jar — 152
72. Ranch Kale Chips — 153
73. Tomatoes (Green For Frying) — 156
74. Tomatoes (Rotel) — 157
75. Tomatoes (Stewed) — 160

Troubleshoot — 164
Yields — 166
Canning Methods — 169
About The Author And Editor — 170

Dedication

Tammy McNeill

I dedicate this work to my parents for teaching me the art of canning and guiding me in life to become the self-sufficient person that I am today enabling me to share this practice with the world.

I began my love of canning as a child, but as an adult, I used it as an escape, therapy as it were. I love teaching children and adults how to take care of themselves without outside help. Properly planning can give one a sense of pride and confidence in their daily life. Living in Michigan gives me many resources as the soil is fertile and there is a wide variety of fruit and veggies that this land bares annually. My three young adopted children are a constant reminder of the need to be frugal and are always my motivation. I am Tammy McNeill, the Author of this cookbook and the creator of "Rebel Canners" a Facebook group that I started a few years ago that has grown by leaps and bounds. I have been amazed at the interest in the concept of being Rebel Canners which embraces the idea that not everything good to can has to be approved by the USDA to be safe which is why we say "Welcome to the dark side." My practice is to preserve time-honored methods that are tried and true. Canning is just something my family did together around the kitchen table when i was young. Our ancestors can teach us about so many things, and I want to pass along everything I have learned to the younger generation.

What Is A "Rebel Canner?"

Many people seem to confuse Rebel Canning with unsafe canning just because we allow the discussion of untested recipes, or the old ways while teaching these techniques, so someone doesn't miss a critical step. One crucial point to understand is if a product is untested that doesn't make it unsafe just not tested. Many foods are untested directly. This is because the government in the US controls the price of certain commodities like pork bellies, milk, butter to name the top three. Store bought food has contamination issues but our small "farm to table" processing does not.

Finally, providing a place where people can learn by asking questions is NOT unsafe. No one dies from asking, "why?" or asking "how" something works. If we don't know the rationale behind the rules, then I have learned nothing. Rebels know the rules better than the "by the book" canners. That is how we know when to bend them and when to keep them. Don't confuse rebel with ignorant or stupid or lazy canners. Most importantly don't confuse them with being unsafe canners. In my opinion, unsafe is not being able to do anything but follow a single book or government agency on canning blindly with no concept of what makes something safe or why a step is critical. Rebel Canners embrace Time-honored methods.

" Learn the rules like a pro so that you can break them like an artist. "– Pablo Picasso

Customize Your Pantry To Last A Year!

Remember you don't have to can these all at once but can build a pantry by canning the bounty in good years and slowly creating a reserve of some items. I try to can a two year supply when fruits have a good season and prices are low, or the neighbors plant too much sweet corn and give me two bushels. It doesn't have to be instant unless you are moving to somewhere far into the woods. I only do one new kind of jelly a year now as we have so many in the pantry to use up. Giving you a choice without having to make a fresh batch of each every year. Building a canning pantry is a process. Learn what you use more of and what you don't like. Can more of what you use.

1. Look at meal planning and jar sizes. For a family of four, usually, quart jars of fruits, juices, and vegetables are good. For jelly and jam, use pints. Canned fish and meat may go in either quarts or pints, but I generally use quarts for my family of four.

For a couple or a single person, consider canning fish and jelly in ½ pint containers (like tuna cans), vegetables and fruits and meats in pints, and juices in quarts.

2. Now figure out how many jars you will need each week.
   - Fruits: 1 per day, except in season equals about 300 quarts.
   - Vegetables: 1 per day, except in season equals about 300 quarts.

The asparagus I can in pint and a half jars it just fits best in the taller jar.
   - Juices: 3 per week equals about 150 quarts.
   - Jelly and jam: 1 per week=52 pints or half pints

(we eat less but gift a lot of these so I will keep this number the same for us)
   - Fish: 1 to 2 per week equals about 100 pints

   (This is usually pints for us not quarts)

- Meat: 1 to 2 per week equals about 100 quarts
- Beans: 75 pints We store our beans dried and can a batch at a time to preserve shelf space. So, if you are going to can for one fruit and vegetable a day, and have some juice, fish, and meat each week, you are already talking 1050 canning jars each year. This list doesn't even cover the ready-made canned foods like soups. It is just a basic needs list. Another example of customizing the list, take pickles I would add a separate category for pickles. For us we use more than 1 quart a week= 52 quarts of just pickled veggies to the above list for my family we go through that and more a year of just pickles. Using only the basic list above a family of four will need 800 quarts, and 325 pints. A single person or couple will need 100 quarts, 775 pints, and 250 ½ pints. My General Rule of Thumb is to have on hand 1000 jars of varying sizes per person for each person above four.

3. Another thing to consider is how much you make in extras. Canning jars, especially smaller ones, are suitable for medicinal salves, for dried herbs and vegetables, and for herb vinegar, etc. I also use a great many quarts and half a gallon for dry good storage. I also can and use a variety of broths an item also not included on the primary list. Ketchup and sauces didn't make "the list" either. There are those sweet extras like deserts with pie fillings, pints of honey and 12 quarts of maple syrup to go on those Dutch apple pancakes.

My friends and family are my inspiration and motivation for all that I do. They are the reason I strive to preserve our food and teach self-sustained living. I want to give an extra special thanks to all the women in my life who believe in me while supporting my dreams while encouraging me to go farther. Karen Stearns was my high school French teacher who taught me much more than a love of language she showed me a lifelong love of learning.

Send a copy/photo of your book receipt to rebelcanners@gmail.com and I will send you a thank you.

I. CONDIMENTS

01. Baby Sauce

Every parent wants the best for their children, so this wholesome and pure sauce is just the ticket.

 Easy

 1 Hour

Ingredients

pears

apple juice or water

Tip: For every 12 pounds of pears then add ¼ cup lemon juice to keep the pear sauce from browning over time. Add it before the last boil in the directions. Or you can just add ¼ teaspoon to each pint jar ½ teaspoon to each quart. For some variety, you can add ½ teaspoon of cinnamon to some of the quarts.

Preparation

Cut the stems and blossom ends off the pears and any bruised areas (unless you are making pear butter then don't worry about the bruises), and any bad spots. Cut into quarters and place in a large pan add a little apple juice or water to the bottom of the pan so as not to burn the pears. Cook down adding more water if needed (juicier pears will start to make their own juice. Once soft run through a Foley food mill. Bring to a boil and turn down the heat. Place in prepared jars. And into the water bath canner (temperature of the water should match that of the jars.) Process in water bath canner for 20 minutes for pints or quarts.

This recipe began in the fall of 1994. It was a very good year for pears. I was given boxes and boxes of pears. They would just appear on my porch like zucchini does from the neighbors and friends. My older two girls didn't like pears. And we needed to do something fast as ripe pears don't keep. So the name was born with my son. Baby sauce. My mother, father and I canned the bounty of pears into pear sauce and called it baby sauce so the kids would try it. Years later when my daughter had kids of her own she asked for the recipe. She said she has never had applesauce that was as tasty as the baby sauce of her childhood… I had to confess my deception. I never lied we made it for Taylor who was a baby at the time hence the name Baby Sauce.

02. Bread and Butter Fiddleheads

This savory pickle gets its flavor as a result of the use of salt instead of sugar in canning this fern.

 Intermediate    3 Hours and 30-minutes

Ingredients

about 4 pounds raw, cleaned and trimmed fiddleheads
3 large onions, thinly sliced
1/2 cup sea salt
cold water
ice cubes
5 cups sugar
5 cups white vinegar
1 ½ teaspoons turmeric
1 ½ teaspoons celery seeds
1 ½ teaspoons mustard seeds

Preparation

Prepare fiddleheads by rinsing thoroughly. Then soak to remove all the brown papery outer coverings. In a clean a clean 8-quart pot add fiddleheads, onions. Dissolve the salt in enough cold water to cover fiddleheads and onions. Then add ice to the water and fiddleheads and onions. Let stand covered in a cool place for 2 hours... Drain and rinse fiddleheads, Add the sugar, vinegar, turmeric, celery seeds and mustard seeds into a separate saucepan. Over high heat, bring to a boil. Add to the fiddleheads and onions and then heat together to a boil. Spoon hot fiddleheads into clean jars and making sure to over fiddleheads with the liquid... Remove any air bubbles that form. Adjust the liquid up to 1/2-inch headspace. Wipe the jar rim. Apply lids and rings. Water bath for 15 minutes. Yield 6 pints.

NOTES:

_____

03. Bread and Butter Pickles

This cross between a sweet pickle and dill has captured the hearts of many. The crisp crunch accompanied with the candy-like texture brings great pleasure to one's pallet. This pickle you must make in large quantities and share.

 Intermediate    3 Hours and 30-minutes

Ingredients

7 cups sugar (can use less)
3 cups white vinegar
2 tablespoons mustard seed
2 teaspoons celery seed
2 teaspoons ground turmeric
6 quarts heaping cucumbers sliced thin
sliced onions
2 green peppers sliced
½ cup sea salt
ice
2 quarts water
3 cloves garlic (remove when you boil)

Preparation

Let cucumbers stand 2 hours with water, salt, and ice. Then drain.

Add vegetables and stir well. Add sugar, vinegar, and spices. Bring to a boil on high heat. Remove garlic. Pour into jars and seal. I water bath mine.

I found this recipe handwritten on an envelope in a recipe book I bought. Tips: Choose long, slender cucumbers. Dark or light green. Yellow ones are not desirable for pickles.

NOTES:
_____
_____
_____
_____
_____
_____
_____
_____

NOTES:

04. Brown Sugar Sauce

This rich sauce is a beautiful replacement for syrup when you need to add a sugary taste to pancakes or waffles.

 Easy

 20-Minutes

Ingredients

2 cups brown sugar
1 cup water
6-8 tablespoons butter
1 teaspoon vanilla (optional)

Preparation

Mix brown sugar and water in a saucepan. Keep stirring it until it comes to a boil to prevent scorching. Boil it for 5 minutes. Turn off the heat. Slowly add the butter and keep stirring until completely melted. You can add 1/2 teaspoon vanilla if you wish (or use imitation maple flavoring.) Use just as you would use maple syrup for instance on pancakes or waffles. Serve it hot. My sister used to make this all the time instead of having maple syrup on hand.

NOTES:

_____
_____
_____
_____
_____
_____
_____

05. Black Bean Dip

This hearty dip brings the guests to the table. The blend of flavors between the chili and black beans is fantastic.

 Easy

 2 Hours

Ingredients

1/2 cup dried black beans in each pint

dice one small green chili in each pint

Preparation

Clean and pick through your beans. Remove any bad ones. Add the beans and chili to each jar. Add ½ teaspoon salt to each jar (optional) fill to one inch head space with water. Apply lids and rings. Process pints for 75 minutes at 10 pounds of pressure. May need to adjust pressure for higher altitudes. To serve open and drain beans reserving the liquid. Blend add liquid to get a thick spread consistency. Serve with tortilla chip made from the flour tortilla recipe found in this cookbook. Makes great bean burritos with soft tortilla shells. Bake with some enchilada sauce and cheese on top.

NOTES:

_____
_____
_____
_____
_____

06. Cowboy Candy

Spicy jalapenos offer their unique flair to create an astoundingly candied delight. Pair this with cream cheese and crackers for a fantastic appetizer.

 Intermediate

 90-Minutes

Ingredients

LARGE BATCH
3 pounds sliced jalapeños
2 cups cider vinegar
6 cups sugar
1/2 teaspoon turmeric
1/2 teaspoon celery seed
1 teaspoon cayenne
3 teaspoons garlic powder

SMALL BATCH
1 pound fresh jalapeños, sliced
2/3 cup apple cider vinegar
2 cups white sugar
2 tablespoons mustard seed
1/4 teaspoon turmeric
1/4 teaspoon celery seed
1 tablespoon garlic powder
1/4 teaspoon cayenne pepper

Preparation

LARGE BATCH
Mix everything except the peppers in a large pan and bring to a boil, boil lightly 5 minutes. Add peppers and boil 5 more minutes, pack in pint jars. Leave ¼ inch headspace. Water bath 15 minutes. Makes six pints. Serve on crackers with cream cheese.

Tips: Wear gloves when slicing the peppers. Do not mix green and red peppers but use all of one color as the two together can make an off colored batch. Leftover brine can be canned and used as a pork or chicken marinade before baking.

SMALL BATCH
Mix apple cider vinegar, sugar, and spices. Bring to a boil. Reduce for 5 minutes to a simmer. Add jalapeños and simmer for additional 5 minutes. Fill jars with jalapeños first and add liquid filling the jars leaving a 1/4 inch headspace. Process in a water bath for 15 minutes. Makes 2 pints.

07. Cranberry Ketchup

Put a tangy twist on a traditional staple with this homemade delight.

 Easy

 90-Minutes

Ingredients

Preparation

4 cups of cranberries, mashed
1 teaspoon cinnamon
1 teaspoon cloves
1 teaspoon allspice
1 teaspoon pepper
2 cups white sugar
1/2 teaspoon sea salt
1 cup white vinegar
dash of cayenne pepper

Mix together in a large saucepan and bring to a full rolling boil. Boil until sauce has thickened. Pour into jelly jars and seal with paraffin wax. Or process in a boiling water bath for 15 minutes. Makes a great way to use up all those cranberries on sale after the holidays.

NOTES:

_____
_____
_____
_____
_____
_____
_____
_____
_____
_____

NOTES:

08. Cranberry Relish

The holidays are an excellent time to share this rare treat with family and friends as it unites fruit creating a burst of flavor with every bite. Make a few extra to give as gifts because you will be the hit of the party with this relish.

 Intermediate    90-Minutes

Ingredients

1 12-ounce package of cranberries, washed
2 small golden delicious apples, cored and grated with the skin on
1 medium orange, seeded and the pit removed
2 cups sugar

Preparation

Grate the orange then zest the peel and save the zest. Cook cranberries in enough water to cover and add 2 cups sugar. Add the fruit and orange zest while allowing it to simmer until it is fully cooked and has a jam-like consistency. Hot pack into pint jars and water bath for 20 minutes.

NOTES:

_____
_____
_____
_____
_____
_____
_____
_____
_____
_____

09. Fireweed Honey

This honey is a mainstay in our house with its zingy taste. The flower is called Fireweed as it grows first in many places after a major fire.

 Intermediate    1 Hour

Ingredients

45 pink clover blossoms
25 white clover blossoms
100 Fireweed blossoms
1 teaspoon alum
10 cups sugar
2 cups water

Preparation

Wash blooms in cold water. Drain. Put all ingredients except alum, sugar, and water into a large pan. Add the water and alum. Let sit for 10 minutes. Bring to a boil and boil until fireweed turns gray and water is a purple color. Strain through cheesecloth or jelly bag. Return flower tea liquid to the pan and add pre-measured sugar. Bring to a rolling boil slowly. Stir constantly. Ladle into prepared canning jars and water bath process for 10 minutes.

NOTES:

_____
_____
_____
_____
_____
_____
_____
_____

NOTES:

10. Flavored Extracts

What a treat it is to use homemade extract that allows you to have confidence in the fresh flavors and their origin.

 Easy

 30-Minutes

Ingredients

VANILLA
5-7 vanilla beans
Vodka or Bourbon Whiskey

MINT
1/2 cup mint leaves

ORANGE
1 orange

LEMON
1 lemon

Preparation

VANILLA:
Choose a nice bottle for gift giving. Add 5-7 vanilla beans after slicing a slit lengthwise in each. Cover with vodka or Bourbon Whiskey. Let set. It only gets betting with age. You can add more alcohol and let set to keep making more extract from the same beans. Eventually, you will need to add more beans. Use high proof alcohol for a better quality vanilla. Not all vanilla beans are created equal so experiment with beans grown in different countries. Note: For a nonalcoholic version use glycerine instead of the vodka. Food grade glycerine is available at cake decorating stores.

MINT:
Follow the same directions as the vanilla extract but substitute washed and dried freshly picked mint leaves (about ½ cup) for the vanilla beans.

ORANGE:
Substitute orange zest of one orange for the vanilla beans in the above recipe for vanilla extract.

LEMON:
Substitute lemon zest of one lemon for the vanilla beans in the above recipe for vanilla extract.

11. Lard, Butter, Bacon

Make the flakiest pie crust with Lard and flavor your cooking with bacon with ease when you plan and preserve.

 Easy

 2 Hours

Ingredients

1) Lard

2) Bacon ends and pieces

3) Unsalted butter or half unsalted mixed with half salted (the salt concentrates so don't use all salted butter.)

Half pint jars, sanitized and kept hot

Note: There is no USDA testing for these recipes.

Note: The USDA doesn't recommend canning butter (but you can buy canned butter in the store.)

Preparation

1) LARD:

Take rendered lard then melt and ladle into prepared hot jars using a funnel. Wipe the rim with a vinegar soaked clean rag. Apply lids and rings. Process 75 minutes pints or 90 minutes quarts at 10 pounds of pressure. You may need to adjust for higher altitudes. To use: This can be used to replace shortening in any recipe. Lard makes the flakiest pie crusts.

2) BACON:

Canning bacon ends and pieces. Brown bacon ends and pieces, pack into pint jars. Process for 75 minutes at 10 pounds of pressure.

3) BUTTER:

Melt butter, Skim off the foam that floats to the top. Stir back in the milk solids up from the bottom Ladle into jars using a funnel. Leave a 1-inch headspace. Wipe the rim with a vinegar soaked clean rag. Apply lids and rings. Process 60 minutes for half pints at 10 pounds of pressure. May need to adjust for higher altitudes. After jars are sealed but still liquid, shake occasionally to mix the milk solids back in as it cools completely. Use caution the melted butter is extremely hot and if a lid comes off you could get burned.

12. Margarine

Coconut oil has found its way into many homes and has gained popularity in today's society. It is a healthy choice when making margarine.

 Easy

 90-Minutes

Ingredients

MARGARINE

1 cup salted butter, softened
1 cup high-quality vegetable oil or coconut oil

PAN GREASING MIXTURE
1 cup flour
1 cup Crisco

Preparation

Blend until thoroughly mixed. Store in the refrigerator. This recipe was given to my mother in law by her cancer doctor. I prefer to avoid hydrogenated oils, so it has evolved over the years to use better quality oils. Tip: 1 cup butter equals a ½ pound. Cream together with a mixer. Put in a tightly covered container. May be stored in the cupboard. Easy to make up before cookie baking time and have on hand. Tip: You can use equal amounts applesauce to replace vegetable oil in any baking recipe to reduce fat. For this reason, alone I can extra pints of applesauce just for baking.

NOTES:

_____
_____
_____
_____

13. Pineapple Topping

This sweet sensation is a great ice cream topping with its delectable taste and perfect texture. A perfect selection for a banana split to add just the right touch. This topping has a million and one uses.

 Intermediate    90-Minutes

Ingredients

5 cups crushed pineapple in juice
4 cups sugar
optional: 1-3 tablespoon Clear Jel if you want to thicken it more after boiling down

Preparation

Boil until sugar is dissolved and sauce thickens about 10 minutes. Ladle into 8 oz canning jars leaving 1/4 inch headspace and process in a boiling water bath 15 minutes. Yield about six 8 oz jars. Boil to the gelling point if you want to make jam.

NOTES:
_____
_____
_____
_____
_____
_____
_____
_____
_____
_____

14. Rose Water Syrup

Have you ever wondered what the key ingredient for Baklava was? Rose water is the secret to that customarily Greek sweet. Now your Baklava will have the authentic element that distinguishes yours from all the rest.

 Easy

 Overnight plus 90-minutes

Ingredients

boiling water
white sugar
¼ teaspoon lemon juice

Preparation

Make a strong tea with fresh-picked rose petals and boiling water. Let sit overnight. Strain. Measure liquid. Bring to a boil and add enough white sugar to make a simple syrup (1 cup sugar to each cup of tea and ¼ teaspoon lemon juice to preserve the color.) Ladle hot syrup into prepared jars. Water bath process in jelly jars 10 minutes. This is a vital ingredient for delicious Baklava.

NOTES:

_____
_____
_____
_____
_____
_____
_____
_____

15. Refrigerator Pickles

Let the magic happen to these cucumbers in the refrigerator where the pickling process takes place.

 Intermediate

 3 Hours and 30-minutes prep plus 2 weeks in the refrigerator.

Ingredients

8 cups cucumbers, sliced thin
1 cup white vinegar
1 tablespoon sea salt
1 cup thinly sliced onions
1 ¾ cups sugar
1 tablespoon celery seed

Preparation

Heat the vinegar and sugar to dissolve the sugar. Let cook and mix all remaining ingredients. Cover with the liquid and let sit 2 weeks covered in the refrigerator. Serve chilled.

NOTES:

_____
_____
_____
_____
_____
_____
_____
_____
_____
_____
_____

16. Sweet Relish

A summer picnic or a party in your backyard is the perfect venue for this wholesome relish or just as an added touch to your favorite dish.

 Intermediate

 Overnight plus 3 hours and 30-minutes

Ingredients

8 large cucumbers, sliced
¼ cup salt
4 sweet red peppers, seeded and cored
4 large onions, quartered
1 ½ tablespoons celery seed
1 ½ tablespoons mustard seed
2 ½ cups sugar
1 ½ cup white vinegar

Preparation

Slice cucumbers into a crock or glass bowl. Add salt and mix well. Let stand overnight in the refrigerator. Drain and force through coarse blade of food chopper with peppers and onions. Put in kettle and add remaining ingredients. Bring to a boil. Cook uncovered occasionally stirring for about 30 minutes. Pack into hot jars and seal. Makes 3 pints or 6 half pints. Tip: Relish can be made with oversize and a few very slightly starting to turn yellowed cucumbers. Tip: No milk in the fridge? Replace 1 cup skim milk with 4 tablespoons nonfat dry milk powder and 1 cup water, mix well.

NOTES:

_____
_____
_____
_____

NOTES:

II. BREADS

17. Baked Pancake

A fast and easy way to make one pancake that serves many. Sunday morning just got a little easier.

 Easy

 45-Minutes

Ingredients

milk
1 cup pancake mix (follow the package directions but use milk as the liquid to make a thick pancake batter.)

To this add:
1 teaspoon vanilla
3 eggs

Preparation

Mix all the ingredients well. Pour into a buttered casserole dish. Bake at 350 degrees until a knife in the center comes out clean. Cut into squares and serve with butter and syrup. This method is much quicker. Makes a sheet cake like pancake.

NOTES:

18. French Toast

Thick toast is the secret to making this eggy treat. Cinnamon and vanilla set this recipe apart from all the others.

 Easy

 45-Minutes

Ingredients

Texas toast (It is a thicker bread so it doesn't get as soggy)
1 1/2-2 eggs per slice of bread
dash milk
dash of cinnamon
very tiny splash of vanilla

Preparation

Dredge in the beaten mixture of eggs and spices fry until golden turn fry on the other side until golden. Serve or freeze to reheat and serve later. May eat with powdered sugar or maple syrup. So here's how to freeze. Place in single layer on a cookie sheet into the freezer, once frozen remove from tray put in ziplock and return to freezer. Take out what's needed leave rest till needed. Tip: Day old bread from the outlet is better for this too (again less soggy) so save some money and buy the cheaper bread at 79-99 cents a loaf to make this a frugal meal. Since french toast was created to use up the stale bread in the first place this is the perfect recipe for that bargain outlet bread.

NOTES:

_____
_____
_____

19. Tortillas (Flour)

Freshly made tortillas are so much better than store bought and your family will love the added touch these make to the tacos we included in this cookbook. Try making your own chips from them.

 Easy  30-Minutes

Ingredients

6 cups flour
1 teaspoon salt
1 tablespoon baking powder
1/2 cup shortening

Preparation

Blend together add about 1 1/2 water add slowly stir roll balls and then roll out on a floured board. Cook on a griddle till lightly brown. Serve with home canned taco meat, home canned beans, and fresh vegetables.

NOTES:
_____
_____
_____
_____
_____
_____
_____
_____
_____
_____
_____

III. DESSERTS

20. Chocolate Pie (Christmas)

The holidays are not the same without this creamy, perfect Oreo pie. Chocolate, chocolate and more chocolate.

 Easy

 1 Hour

Ingredients

1 chocolate Oreo crust
1 cup mini chocolate chips
1 cup white mini marshmallows
1 package non instant chocolate pudding

Preparation

In the bottom of the crust spread out the chocolate chips in a layer. Next layer about half way up with the mini marshmallows. Cook puddings according to package directions. Pour gently into pie crust careful not to move the layers too much. Refrigerate. Serve chilled.

NOTES:

_____
_____
_____
_____
_____
_____
_____
_____
_____

21. Christmas Finger Jell-O

Jell-O has a texture of its own and adds color one's table at any venue so celebrate and show your originality.

 Easy

 45-Minutes

Ingredients

Red and green Jell-O packages and makes two batches
3 boxes any one color and flavor
3 cups boiling water
1 cup cold water
4 envelopes unflavored gelatin
1 cup water
2 tablespoons lemon juice

Preparation

Dissolve jello in the boiling water. Dissolve gelatin in cold water in a separate bowl. Mix the two together. Add lemon juice. Pour into a deep pan. Chill in refrigerator. Cut into squares. Serve chilled.

NOTES:

22. Rum Cake

This cake lasts a very long time when kept in the refrigerator. Rum in the glaze and cake creates a smooth taste.

 Easy  2 Hours

Ingredients

CAKE
1 cup chopped walnuts or pecans
1 box yellow cake mix (without pudding)
4 eggs
1/2 cup oil
1/2 cup rum
1/2 cup water

GLAZE
1 cup sugar
1 stick butter
1/2 cup Rum

Preparation

CAKE
Combine all. Drop by large teaspoonfuls onto greased cookie sheet. Chopped Walnuts or pecans in the bottom of a greased Bundt Pan. Stir together and pour into a Bundt pan. Bake at 325 degrees for 50-60 minutes. Cool the cake for at least 5-10 minutes before adding glaze.

GLAZE
Let cake cook completely before you dump it out of the pan. Boil 3 minutes. Pour over cake that is cooled for 5-10 minutes. You can poke holes into the cake with a fork to help penetration through the cake. Serve with Cool Whip. This cake gets better the longer it sits. I wrap it in aluminum foil and it keeps for a month in the refrigerator.

NOTES:

_____

_____

23. Strawberry Rhubarb Pie Filling

Strawberries complement the rhubarb bringing a sweetness to this classic pie filling.

 Intermediate    2 Hours

Ingredients

3 large apples peeled and finely chopped (I don't peel mine)
1 tablespoon orange zest
1/4 cup fresh squeezed orange juice (optional I don't use in mine I used apple juice)
7 cups of 1 inch slices of rhubarb
2 cups sugar
4 cups of halved, and hulled strawberries

Preparation

Cook rhubarb, apples, juice, and zest. Bring to a boil over medium-high heat. Stirring frequently until rhubarb is tender about 12 minutes. Add strawberries and return to a boil. Remove from heat. Ladle into hot jars leaving 1" headspace. Adjust caps and lids. Process in a boiling water Bath for 15 minutes. Remove canner lid and wait 5 min then remove jars, Cool, and store. Note: None of this made it into pies as we ate it as an ice cream topping. Tip: White sugar keeps a long time and so does molasses. So never store brown sugar again. It gets hard over time (although mom always puts a crust of bread in with hers to keep it moist.) Instead, make your own brown sugar as you need it. Use 5 cups white sugar. Add molasses 1 tablespoon at a time whisk until well blended. The more molasses the darker the brown sugar. Keep adding until you get the blend that tastes right to you...

24. Thumbprint Cookies

Use your imagination when creating these cookies as the choice of jam dictates the taste. A variety of flavors can be made to please the masses.

 Easy

 90-Minutes

Ingredients

1 ¼ cup butter, softened
1 cup brown sugar
2 eggs
4 cups flour
1 half pint home canned jam

Preparation

Combine brown sugar and butter, add eggs one at a time then add flour 1 cup at a time. Roll into 1-2 inch ball, make a thumbprint in the center, fill with your favorite jam and bake 8-10 minutes at 350 degrees. I use my leftover home canned cranberry relish from Thanksgiving to fill mine for Christmas. It is a tart contrast to all the overly sweet cookies and always the first to leave the cookie trays I make. These are also a great way to use up the last of the jam in the fridge so you have an excuse to open a new jar of another flavor.

NOTES:

_____
_____
_____
_____
_____
_____

25. Zucchini Cookies

This wholesome cookie is a great way to get your veggies while experiencing the sweetness from the raisins and or chocolate if you prefer.

 Easy

 90-Minutes

Ingredients

1 cup grated zucchini

1 cup sugar

½ cup butter or margarine

1 egg, beaten

2 cups flour

1 teaspoon baking powder

1 teaspoon cinnamon

½ teaspoon cloves

1 cup raisins or nuts or chocolate chips (optional)

Preparation

Cream sugar and shortening. Add egg. Slowly add dry ingredients will stirring. Chill 2 hours. Drop by teaspoonfuls on a greased cookie sheet. Preheat oven to 375 degrees. Bake 12 minutes. Tip: These cookies are also good with grated carrot. Or a mix of zucchini and carrots for bright color. Make ahead and freeze for Christmas. An excellent way to use up those extra large zucchinis.

NOTES:

_____
_____
_____
_____
_____
_____
_____
_____
_____

IV. FRUITS

26. Cranberry Juice

The nutrients found in this berry helps fight off many infections while boosting ones overall health.

 Intermediate

 2 Hours plus 4-6 weeks

Ingredients

cranberries
1/2 cup sugar per quart
water
orange zest (optional)

Preparation

Cranberry juice is one of the healthiest drinks. It is so easy to make cranberry juice. Cranberry juice is one of the healthiest drinks. Buy cranberries on sale during the holidays. Add 1 to 1 3/4 cup cranberries in each clean quart jar. Add up to 1/2 cup sugar per quart. (less sugar if you like a tarter juice.) Fill with boiling water to the inch headspace line. Place lids and rings on the jar. Wipe the rims first you have any spill on the rim. Process in boiling water bath for 25 minutes or PC (pressure cook) for 10 minutes at 10 pound of pressure (may need to adjust for higher altitudes.) Wait as long as you can before opening to allow the juice to form in the jar about 4-6 weeks. Shake before opening. Note: Three 12 oz. bags yield about 6 quarts. You can add some orange zest for little orange zing in your juice. Tip: If you want to make sugar free cranberry juice increase berries to 2 cups and omit the sugar.

27. Pumpkin (Cubed)

Pie, bread, soup, cake and baby food are just a few of the uses of pumpkin. Having it on hand makes it easy to produce these items at the drop of a hat.

 Easy

 3 Hours and 30-minutes

Ingredients

Pumpkin

Preparation

Wash the fruit then remove the seeds and the pulp. Cut the pumpkin into 1 inch wide slices, and peel. Option: Can be cooked unpeeled and peeled after if you choose. It is easy to peel after. Cut flesh into 1-inch cubes. Boil 2 minutes in water. Fill jars with pumpkin cubes and cooking liquid, leaving a 1-inch headspace. Put on lids and tighten. Hot pack in pints or quarts. Leave 1-inch headspace. Apply lids and rings. Process for 55 min pints or 90 min quart at 10 pounds of pressure. May need to adjust for higher altitude. Note: For making pies, drain jars and strain or sieve cubes. Then mash or puree after opening to use.

NOTES:

_____
_____
_____
_____
_____

28. Pumpkin Seeds

You can use the entire pumpkin even down to the seeds that are a salty snack and handy delicacy.

 Easy

 30-Minutes

Ingredients

pumpkin seeds

Preparation

Drying seeds and roasting seeds are two different processes. To dry, carefully wash pumpkin seeds to remove the clinging fibrous pumpkin tissue. Pumpkin seeds can be dried in the sun, in a dehydrator at 115-120 degrees for 1 to 2 hours, or in an oven on warm for 3 to 4 hours. Stir them frequently to avoid scorching. To roast, take dried pumpkin seeds, toss with oil and/or salt and roast in a preheated oven at 250 degrees for 10 to 15 minutes.

NOTES:

_____
_____
_____
_____
_____
_____
_____

29. Rhubarb Fruit Leather

Children and adults alike crave the texture and simplicity of this treat.

 Easy　　　 30-Minutes

Ingredients

about 4 cups rhubarb, chopped in small pieces
boiling water
½ cup brown sugar
1 teaspoon ground cinnamon

Preparation

In a large pan cover the rhubarb with boiling water and let steep for ten minutes. Drain and puree rhubarb in a blender. Add brown sugar and cinnamon. Mix well. Spread on your dehydrators silicone sheet in a thin layer. Dehydrate (135*f) for about 6-8 hours.

Tip: Never cut rhubarb pull and twist to harvest. This way the plant knows to grow a new stem.

NOTES:

_____
_____
_____
_____
_____
_____
_____
_____
_____
_____
_____

V. JELLY, JAM & BUTTERS

30. Apple Butter

Butters bring out the flavor in rolls, toast, burgers, sauces, ice cream, bread, and is a beautiful gift to give to friends.

 Intermediate

 2 Hours plus overnight

Ingredients

4 quarts of apples, cored
2 quarts apple cider
2 cups sugar
1 teaspoon cinnamon
1 teaspoon mace
¾ teaspoon allspice

Preparation

Boil the cider slowly until it reduces to one quart. Add the apples and cook until soft. Run through a foley mill to puree. Place juice, apples, spices, and sugar in an uncovered crockpot overnight on low. Taste. Adjust spices if necessary. If a spoon stands up in it then apple butter is done if still too runny to stand a spoon cook down longer. The secret to a really good apple butter is the variety of apples. It needs at least ¼ granny smith or tart apples and ¼ yellow delicious or equivalent very sweet apples. The other ½ should be a blend of apple varieties. Use a generous variety of apples the better the end product. I myself stay away from the Macintosh. I am looking for a richer meatier sauce and find them better suited to pies. I guess you could say I am an apple snob since I spent my summers at my families apple orchard picking fruit and testing out the old and new varieties. You can also cheat and use applesauce in place of the apples and cider in this recipe and skip ahead to the crockpot steps. Note: The runnier the sauce you start with the longer the cooking time.

31. Pumpkin Butter

Whether it be in a cocktail, granola, candy or just on bread the flavor in this butter will enhance every item you use it in.

 Intermediate  4 Hours

Ingredients

2 cups pumpkin puree
1 teaspoon cinnamon
1/4 teaspoon nutmeg
1/2 teaspoon ginger
1/8 teaspoon cloves
1 cup brown sugar
1 cup white sugar

Note: Pureed pumpkin is no longer recommend by the USDA. They state "It is better to freeze pumpkin butters or mashed squash."

Preparation

Tip: If you don't have brown sugar you can use white sugar and molasses to make brown sugar. One cup of white sugar and one tablespoon of molasses. Mix well. Makes one cup of brown sugar. Combine all in slow cooker mix well. Cook on high covered for 3 hours stirring occasionally. Ladle into pint jars. Refrigerate or Process for 40 minutes water bath or for 20 min at 10 pounds pressure. Adjust pressure to your altitude.

NOTES:
_____
_____
_____
_____
_____
_____
_____
_____

32. Strawberry Jam

Some uses for jam are tarts, popsicles, frostings, muffins, ice cream, cheesecake, even in the Thumbprint cookies found in this cookbook.

 Intermediate    3 Hours

Ingredients

¼ cup lemon juice
5 cups mashed strawberries and liquid (can use frozen)
7 cups sugar (pre-measured and set in a bowl aside)
8 tablespoons powdered pectin
the zest of a lemon

Preparation

Place in strawberries in a large saucepan then add lemon juice. Stir in pectin. Bring mixture to a full rolling boil and add sugar to the berries. Stir it in slowly. Bring to a rolling boil. May add a pat of butter to reduce foaming. Boil at a full rolling boil for two minutes. Place into prepared size jars. Wipe rims with a damp towel. Apply lids and rings. Place in a water bath canner with hot water. Water bath for 10 minutes in the water bath canner. Note: This jam makes a great topping for ice cream, too!

NOTES:

_____
_____
_____
_____
_____
_____

33. Tipsy Peach Jam

Peach Schnapps and fresh peaches create a sensational jam that you will simply have to share. Once your friends and family taste the creative combination found in this tipsy treat, they will all want a jar or two.

 Intermediate    3 Hours

Ingredients

12 fresh peaches, peeled, pitted and chopped
4 1/2 cups white sugar
8 tablespoons powdered pectin
2 tablespoons Peach Schnapps per pint jar

Preparation

Put chopped peaches in the bottom of a large saucepan. Bring to a low boil, and cook for about 20 minutes or until peaches become liquid, Pour peaches into a bowl, and then measure 6 cups back into the pan. Add sugar, and bring to a boil over medium heat. Gradually stir in dry pectin, and bring to a full rolling boil for 1 minute longer. Remove from heat after 1 minute, and transfer to pint jars. Add the Schnapps. Wipe the rims. Apply lids and rings. Process in hot water bath canner for 10 minutes. Each year I make a different jam or jelly to try. Tipsy Peaches say 1994 me, the year my son was born. It was also a very good year for peaches in our area. I always can with Red Haven Peaches. The trick to easy peach canning is to always buy freestone, not clingstone type peaches. They make for pretty slices. But for jams and jelly, you can use cling as you are going to hack and chop them any way they do not have to look pretty. But if they are available and the same price goes with the less effort freestone varieties for canning.

34. Cherry Jam

You can use your imagination when it comes to the blend of cherries that you choose for this jam.

 Intermediate

 2 Hours

Ingredients

4 cups wild cherries (Wild Choke, Pin, Black Cherries) with their juice (that have been cooked slightly to soften and then run through a Foley mill to remove the pits)

4 ¾ cups sugar (pre-measured and set in a bowl aside)

8 tablespoons powdered pectin

the zest of one lemon or 2 tablespoons dehydrated lemon zest

Preparation

Place fruit in a large saucepan next adding the lemon zest. Stir in pectin. Bring mixture to a full rolling boil then add sugar to the fruit juices. Stir it in slowly. Bring to a rolling Boil. You may add a pat of butter to reduce foaming. Boil at a full rolling boil for two minutes. Place into prepared size jars. Wipe rims with a damp towel. Apply lids and rings. Place in a water bath canner with hot water. Water bath for 10 minutes in the water bath canner. Note: This jam makes a great topping for ice cream.

NOTES:

_____
_____
_____
_____
_____
_____

35. Apple Cider Jelly

Cider makes this jelly easy to prepare and I love the use of red hots as they create fabulous color and flavor it in a way that no other spices can do.

 Intermediate    2 Hours

Ingredients

1-quart apple cider
2/3 cup red hots heart candy (optional)
1 (1 ¾ ounce) package powdered fruit pectin
5 cups granulated sugar

Preparation

Place apple cider, red hots and pectin in a large kettle, and bring to a full rolling boil. Add sugar. Return to a full rolling boil, stirring constantly. Boil for 1 minute. Remove from heat, skim off any foam. Pour into hot jars, leaving 1/4 inch headspace. Adjust caps. Process for 10 minutes in a boiling water bath. Makes about 6 half-pints. Note: Good as a glaze on pork chops or ham also.

NOTES:

_____
_____
_____
_____
_____
_____
_____
_____

36. Elderberry Jelly

This beautiful, fragrant, bitter, blue-black berry provides an opportunity to ingest a product that encourages a self-sustained and wildcrafting lifestyle. The benefits are endless and the taste divine.

 Intermediate  90-Minutes

Ingredients

JELLY
3 cups elderberry juice (Juice recipe in this book.)
¼ cup lemon juice
7 cups sugar (pre measured and set in a bowl
8 tablespoons powdered pectin (1 package)

Preparation

Place in juice in a large saucepan. Add lemon juice. Stir in pectin. Bring mixture to a full rolling boil. Add sugar to the juice. Stir it in slowly. Bring to a rolling Boil. May add a pat of butter to reduce foaming (optional.) Boil at a full rolling boil for two minutes. Place into prepared size jars. Wipe rims with damp towel. Apply lids and rings. Place in a water bath canner with hot water. Bathe them for 5 minutes in the water bath canner. One year in the 1990s I picked so many elderberries I canned 145 pints of elderberry jelly for my Aunt Harriet. It is still one of my favorites. My mother told the story that during the war my grandfather worked at the sugar factory and just before the start of WWII he purchased several large bags of sugar for the family. He hid them under the stairs in the house. So they had jelly sandwiches to take to school instead of lard sandwiches like so many their friends. Grandma had elderberry bushes in front of her house and more than once she ran off people out to pick her elderberries during the lean times of WW2 the cooked elderberries taste like blueberry almost to me.

37. Apple Jelly (without added pectin)

We love this Apply Jelly made without added pectin. It is essential to know to use firm fruit as they are naturally pectin enriched.

 Intermediate    4 Hours

Ingredients

JUICE
4 cups apple juice (about 3 pounds apples and 3 cups water)
2 tablespoons strained lemon juice if desired
3 cups sugar

Preparation

TO PREPARE THE JUICE
First, you must sort, wash, and remove ends but do not peel or core from the apples (OR use the saved peels and cores from other apple canning projects.) Cut into small pieces. Add water, cover, and bring to boil on high heat. Reduce heat and simmer for 30 minutes, or until apples are soft. Strain juice. Makes or 5 half-pint jars.

TO MAKE THE JELLY
Measure 4 cups of apple juice into a kettle. Add lemon juice and sugar and stir well. Boil over high heat until jelly mixture sheets from a spoon. Remove from heat and skim off foam. Pour hot jelly immediately into hot, jars, leaving ¼ inch headspace. Wipe rims of jars. Apply lids and rings. Process in a boiling water bath for 15 minutes.

NOTES:
_____

38. Dandelion Jelly

Kidney stones, liver and bile issues can cause significant discomfort to one's body. It also aids in the treatment of appetite loss. Dandelion has natural benefits in helping many skin conditions and diuretic problems.

 Intermediate

 Overnight plus 2 Hours

Ingredients

dandelion flowers

1-quart jar of tea
1 box of pectin
juice of 1/2 a lemon

Preparation

TEA

For dandelion tea pick the flowers and cover with boiling water. This tastes like honey. To make dandelion tea pick the flowers and pour boiling water over them. Let the tea stand overnight to steep. Strain. You can stop here and can the tea for jelly making later. Place in quart jars and water bath can for 10 minutes.

JELLY

To make jelly just open and use 1-quart jar of tea, 1 box of pectin, the juice of 1/2 a lemon. Bring to a boil, add 4 cups of sugar and bring back to a full rolling boil for one minute. Place in jelly jars and process for 5 min in water bath.

NOTES:

_____

_____

_____

39. Elderberry Juice

Do you suffer from headaches or heart pain? Possibly you have Influenza. This juice is a natural remedy for many afflictions so explore the uses after making your batch.

 Intermediate

 2 Hours plus overnight

Ingredients

elderberries
sugar (optional: Splenda)

Preparation

TO PREPARE THE JUICE
Stem the elderberries using a fork. Mash with a potato masher. Place in a large saucepan. Heat gently until they become juicy. Turn to low heat and simmer with a cover for 15 minutes. Let stand till cool. Place in cheesecloth and let the juice drain out over a bowl do not squeeze for a clearer juice. If you don't mind a cloudy juice then squeeze away for more juice. I tied my cheese cloth bag to a broom handle and let set over a five gallon pail overnight for every last drop. Refrigerate to use right away or water bath can for 15 minutes pints 20 minutes quarts.

DRINKING JUICE
To make elderberry juice for drinking add between 1/4 to 3 cups sugar (to taste) to every 6-7 cups juice before canning. Or 7 cups juice and 1/2 cup Stevia or Splenda for a sugar-free juice. Note: It takes about 25 pounds of elderberries to make 7 quarts or 16 pounds to make 9 pints. Tip: A fork is the easiest way to strip the berries off the stems.

40. Elderberry Syrup (Basic)

This natural detoxifier can boost one's immunity lessen cold symptoms and assist in the control of blood sugar. Kids like the taste which helps when treating children that share illness.

 Intermediate    3 Hours

Ingredients

juice from fresh elderberries or dried berries
1/4 to 3 cups sugar (to taste) to every 6-7 cups

sugar-free version:
7 cups juice and 1/2 cup Stevia or Splenda for a sugar-free juice.

Preparation

Make juice from fresh elderberries. Sort berries and remove stems and any unripe berries. Place in large saucepan. Add enough water to cover and bring to a rapid boil and then turn heat down to a simmer and simmer for 20-30 minutes. Skins should pop open. Crush the berries with a potato masher. Let simmer longer up to an hour. Liquid should be a deep dark purple. Strain out the berries. Tip: You can dehydrate berries, to make a powder that can be added to smoothies. Can the juice in pints to make syrup later by water bath 10 minutes for pints or quarts and 20 minutes for half gallons. Use one pint to make a batch of syrup at a time in place of the water and dried berries in the recipe below. Or use the quarts to make elderberry jelly following the recipe on the Sure Gel package. If you don't have fresh berries follow the recipe below for dried berries which can be purchased online.

41. Wild Violet Jelly

Need relief from that nagging cough? This health-giving, almost peppery tasting treatment efficiently assists in purifying one's blood and acts as an immune system booster.

 Easy

 3 Hours

Ingredients

2 cups wild violets
2 cups boiling water
juice of 1 lemon (strained)
4 cups sugar
1 package powdered sugar

VIOLET SYRUP
4 cups of wild violet flowers
6 cups boiling water
2 1/2 cups of sugar (per cup of liquid)

Preparation

JELLY: 2 cups wild violets (purple violets are best but a few whites are ok) stems removed. Pour 2 cups boiling water over clean petals. Cover and steep in the refrigerator for 24 hours. Strain the juice and discard the flower petals. Add strained juice of 1 lemon. Jelly will turn a nice light pink color. Add 4 cups sugar, boil 1 min, add 1 package powdered sugar, bring to full boil for 2 minutes. Stir and skim off foam. Pour into sterilized jelly jars. Cover and process in 10 minutes in boiling water bath. Note: These are not the houseplants your grandmother had on the window sill. As with all wild plants do your own research and be sure you can identify them correctly. Tip: Violets are said to have cough suppressant attributes. So this is the perfect spring jelly. Note: You can use this same process with other edible flowers to make various jellies in turn. You can also freeze the flowers until you have enough to make the tea.

SYRUP: 4 cups of wild violet flowers to 6 cups boiling water, let sit overnight, covered. Strain out petals. For every cup of liquid add 2 1/2 cups of sugar. Put into a boiling water bath for 20 minutes. I use this personally as a mild cough syrup for myself and my kids. Tip: 8 tablespoons powdered pectin equals one store-bought box of pectin.

VI. MEATS

42. Hot Dogs

Base ball, hot dogs, apple pie and muscle cars are part of our American tradition.

 Easy    2 Hours

Ingredients

high-grade meat hot dogs

Preparation

Start with high grade meat hot dogs with minimal fillers.

Poke holes with a fork into each. In pint and a half or quart jars stuff in hot dogs so they are standing up right. Fill to one inch head space with water. Apply lids and rings. Process at 10 pounds of pressure for 90 minutes. May need to adjust pressure to your altitude.

Optional: for spicier hot dogs add a small Tabasco chili pepper that has had a slit sliced lengthwise in it to each jar before processing.

NOTES:

_____
_____
_____
_____
_____

43. Chicken Bone Broth

Creating a good stock broth to be used in your recipes is an essential part of cooking. The challenge is to get a hearty flavor that will enhance all of them. Now your leftovers will take on a new life.

 Easy    2 Hours

Ingredients

CHICKEN
turkey and rotisserie chicken or Rabbit
garlic
onions
potato peels
carrot peels

BEEF
beef bones
vegetable scraps
onions (diced)
carrots (diced)

VEGGIE
canned water

Preparation

CHICKEN: You might have a canning addiction when you ask friends to save the carcasses for you. Turkey and rotisserie chicken in the stock pot with garlic cloves. It's gonna be some cold busting broth in our house. Save the leftover chicken, turkey and rabbit carcasses from other meals. Also, save the skins of garlic and onions. A few potato and carrot peels will work too but may darken the broth to almost a dirty brown color. You can just use entire garlic cloves as well. Simmer until you get a rich deep broth. Strain. Place in quart jars and pressure can for 30 minutes at 10 pounds of pressure. You may need to adjust for higher altitudes.

BEEF: Roast bones in the oven slightly until browned. Remove from oven. Add vegetable scraps as well as carrots and onions diced. Cover with water and simmer until a dark rich broth is obtained. Strain. Place in quart jars and pressure can for 30 minutes at 10 pounds of pressure. You may need to adjust for higher altitudes. Note: I saved the juice I drained off the corn I make for supper and add it to the stock for a nice rich color. I keep a bucket in the freezer of vegetable trimmings and skins to use for making my broths. This is also the basis for my vegetable broth. But remember too many potato peels give a dark dirty color to broths.

44. Chicken and Dumplings

Grandmas and grandpas, moms and dads, aunts and uncles have warmed the hearts and tummies of their loved ones with this satisfying dish for generations. I call this fast food!

 Easy

 45-Minutes

Ingredients

STEW
1 quart of home canned chicken soup starter (recipe in this book)
1 quart of water or chicken broth
1 teaspoon poultry seasoning
1 teaspoon sea salt (optional)
1/2 teaspoon ground pepper (optional)
1 bay leaf (optional)

DUMPLINGS
1 cup flour
2 teaspoons baking powder
1/2 teaspoon sea salt (optional)
1/2 cup milk (or water, but milk is better)
1 tablespoon parsley flakes (optional)

Preparation

STEW
This is my go-to meal when I don't feel like cooking but we are cold and hungry. It is super quick and easy. This is my idea of fast food. Bring to a boil on the stove in a large 5 quart stock pan with a lid. While the stew is coming up to a boil mix the dumplings.

DUMPLINGS
Stir together flour, baking powder, sugar, parsley and salt in medium-size bowl. Stir in milk to make a soft dough. Drop by teaspoon spoonfuls into boiling chicken and broth. Remember that they will swell up and get larger so don't start out making them too big. The bigger the dumplings the longer it takes to cook them. Cover and simmer about 15 minutes without lifting the lid. Tip: The dumplings can be made ahead and frozen too.

45. Chicken Soup Starter

The therapeutic uses found in chicken soup dates back to 60 AD when a book called "De Materia Medica" identifies its benefits. An Army surgeon of Emperor Nemo called Pedacius Dioscorides wrote about its virtues in his book.

 Easy

 2 Hours

Ingredients

Chicken, diced in large pieces
Broth (Made from the chicken bones, onion skins, celery ends, carrot peels)
carrots, diced small
celery, diced small
onion, diced small (optional)
1-2 cloves garlic, finely chopped (optional)

Preparation

Place in quart jars and pressure cook 90 minutes at 10 pounds of pressure (adjust pressure to your altitude) or pints for 75 minutes at 10 pounds of pressure (adjust for your altitude.) Note: This works really well with leftover turkey.

NOTES:
_____
_____
_____
_____
_____
_____
_____
_____
_____
_____
_____
_____

46. Corned Beef Hash

Corned Beef is the dish that they served at the Inaugural Dinner of Abraham Lincoln. Hash marries potatoes, onions and Corned Beef producing a delightful medley.

 Intermediate  2 Hours

Ingredients

10 pounds Corned Beef, rinsed in cold water
10 large size potatoes, peeled and diced
2 large onions, diced
boiling water

Preparation

Chop and dice the corned beef into 1-inch cubes. Start by filling the pint jars with 1/4 full of potatoes and onions. Then fill to 1 1/2-inch headspace with Corned Beef. I don't add salt as I find corned beef salty enough already. Add boiling water filling to 1-inch headspace. Clean off the rims before placing the lids and rings. 75 minutes at 10 pounds for pints or 90 minutes at 10 pounds pressure if you are making quarts. Adjust pressure to your altitude. The corned beef is easy to find after St Patrick's Day marked down on sale. Yield about 14 pints.

NOTES:

_____
_____
_____
_____
_____

47. Corned Venison

Tenderizing your Venison will ensure satisfactory texture.

 Easy    2 Hours

Ingredients

8-pounds wild game brisket
2 quarts water
1 cup kosher salt
1/2 cup white vinegar
4 tablespoons sugar
3-4 bay leaves
1 teaspoon whole black peppercorns
1/2 teaspoon mustard seed
pinch ground cloves
4 coarsely minced garlic cloves

Preparation

Trim the brisket of as much fat as you desire. Fat is where the flavor is, so do not trim all the fat off. Place the sealed bag in the refrigerator for one week. Turn the bag every other day. Remove the brisket from the bag, and discard the brine. Cook, freeze, or can. For canning process for 75 minutes pints 90 minutes quarts at 10 pounds of pressure. May need to adjust pressure for higher altitudes. Note: The recipe is also suitable for other wild game meats and beef.

NOTES:

_____
_____
_____
_____
_____
_____
_____

48. Ham and Cheese Ball (Christmas)

Family and friends will talk about this on their way to your house for Christmas in great anticipation. The creaminess of the cheddar and cream cheese with the full flavor of ham creates a fantastic experience.

 Easy

 90-Minutes

Ingredients

1 pound slivered ham chopped fine
16 oz cream cheese
2 teaspoons of milk
2 dashes Worcestershire Sauce
12 oz shredded cheddar cheese (or more)
4-8 finely diced green onions

Preparation

Mix cheeses, milk, and Worcestershire sauce. Slowly add in the onion until thoroughly mixed. Roll into a ball and roll in more cheese. Cover with plastic wrap. Chill. Serve with crackers.

NOTES:
_____
_____
_____
_____
_____
_____
_____
_____
_____
_____

49. Ham (Deviled)

Homemade bread compliments this devilish dish, even on a bed of lettuce enticing a burst of savoriness.

 Easy    2 Hours

Ingredients

ham (cubed)
celery (chopped)
onions (diced)
mayonnaise

Preparation

Cube ham add chopped celery and diced onions put in food processor and chop until fine. Fill jars to one-inch headspace. Those tiny jelly jars work well and are the same as pint times. 75 minutes at 10 pounds of pressure. May need to adjust pressure for higher altitude. To use: Open jar add mayonnaise to a spreadable consistency and a dash of mustard. Pepper to taste. Serve between bread slices or on crackers.

NOTES:

_____
_____
_____
_____
_____
_____
_____
_____
_____

50. Ham Loaf

Creating a loaf from ham transcends this meat while the glazes enhance its natural tastiness.

 Easy

 2 Hours

Ingredients

pounds ham loaf mixture (1 pound ground ham, 1 pound lean ground pork)
1/2 cup rolled oats
slices of bread soaked in 1/2 cup milk
egg
1/2 cup onions

GLAZE FOR TOP
1 1/2 cups brown sugar
1/4 cup vinegar
1/2 cup water
teaspoon dry mustard
1/2 cup pineapple juice

Preparation

Shape meat and other ingredients into a loaf. Bake at 350 degrees for 1 1/2 hours or until done. Pour glaze over the top of loaf and baste while cooking.

NOTES:
_____
_____
_____
_____
_____
_____
_____
_____
_____
_____
_____
_____

51. Ham (Omelette)

Having ham at the ready gives you a more extensive range of choices and when it is time to make an omelet.

 Easy

 2 Hours

Ingredients

ham
green peppers
onion

Preparation

Cut leftover ham into small cubes. Place in a small jelly jar. You may add leftover veggies you like in omelets (I do not recommend broccoli) like green pepper or onion finely chopped. Add water to one-inch headspace.process as per pints 75 minutes at 10 pounds pressure. May have to adjust pressure for higher altitude.

NOTES:

_____
_____
_____
_____
_____
_____
_____
_____
_____
_____

52. Pork Roast

My mom often cooked this in the pressure cooker for Sunday dinners when I was a youngster.

 Easy

 3 Hours

Ingredients

Preparation

1 boneless pork loin, Cut into large cubes (about 1 pound per quart jar)
red potatoes, peeled and chopped into quarters
carrots, peeled and cut into large cubes
onions, chopped into large chunks
sea salt
pepper

Fill each jar about ½ full with meat, add a layer of potatoes, a layer of carrots and a few onion pieces. Fill the jar with water to one-inch headspace. Wipe the rims. Add 1 teaspoon salt per wide-mouth quart jar. Add ¼ teaspoon pepper to each if desired. Apply lids and rings. Process pints for 75 minutes at 10 pounds of pressure or quarts for 90 minutes. May need to adjust pressure for higher altitude. To serve open and heat.

NOTES:

_____
_____
_____
_____
_____
_____
_____

53. Sweet and Sour Chicken

Cook some rice and open up a jar soon you'll find yourself enjoying peppers, pineapple and tender chicken. My authentic egg roll recipe from Taiwan brings an age-old appeal to this meal.

 Easy

 2 Hours

Ingredients

4-5 pounds deboned skinless meat cut into bite-size chunks
3 large red and green peppers chopped large
2 small onions chopped large
3 (20 ounce) cans pineapple chunks, drained but reserve the juice
3/4 cups brown sugar
1 1/4 cups white vinegar
6 tablespoons soy sauce
4 tablespoons ketchup
1 teaspoon ginger

Preparation

Layer the chicken, peppers, and onion in quart jars. Heat the remaining ingredients plus 3 cups of the pineapple juice. Bring to a slow boil, dissolve the sugar. Pour liquid into each jar to the 1-inch headspace line. Pressure can for 90 minutes at 10 pounds of pressure. May need to adjust for higher altitude. To serve: Open jars and heat on the stove. Serve over cooked rice. See recipe for Laura's egg rolls following this recipe in our cookbook.

NOTES:
_____
_____
_____
_____
_____
_____
_____

54. Laura's Egg Rolls

Born in Taiwan this recipe made its way to American and now into this cookbook. These simply can't be beat.

 Intermediate    2 Hours

Ingredients

8 packages egg roll wrappers
2-3 pounds of grated carrots
2-8 ounce bags of bean sprouts
8 bunches of green onions diced
5-3/4 pound hamburger
3 pounds pork sausage
3 tablespoons ginger, minced
5 cloves of garlic, diced
2 tablespoons soy sauce
2 tablespoons Chinese 5 spice
1-2 eggs, beaten
vegetable oil for deep frying

Preparation

Cook and drain the meat. Add to vegetables and spices. Take a raw egg (beaten) and go around the edges of the egg wrappers. Fill and roll tightly. Deep fry in vegetable oil until wrappers are golden. Set on paper towel to drain and cool then freeze. You cannot make too many of these! They are so good and good for you too. This recipe was taught to me by my cousin Ray. It was her Taiwanese mother's but my own mother adapted it to our tastes. One thing we never adapted is the amount because you can't make too many.

NOTES:

_____
_____
_____
_____
_____

55. Taco Seasoning and Taco Meat

Meat like this only gets better after being canned. Find our flour tortilla recipe in the bread section of our book.

 Easy

 2 Hours

Ingredients

SEASONING
2 teaspoons chilli powder
1 ½ teaspoons paprika
1 teaspoon onion powder
½ teaspoon garlic powder
½ teaspoon ground cumin
½ teaspoon ground oregano
½ teaspoon fresh ground pepper
½ teaspoon sea salt

TACO MEAT
ground Meat
taco seasoning
optional: onion (diced)

Preparation

SEASONING

Mix well. I like to use my own dehydrated garlic powder and chili powder. Makes enough to season 1 pound of meat.

TACO MEAT

Brown ground meat (2 pounds burger for each quart desired)

Add taco seasoning (about 2 tablespoons per quart more if you like it spicier) and add finely diced onion (optional.) Pack hot into jars. Add 1 teaspoon per quart (or 1/2 teaspoons per pint jar) sea salt. Add water to the headspace. Apply the lids and rings. Process 75 minutes at 10 pounds of pressure for pints or 90 minutes for quarts. May need to adjust the pressure for higher altitudes. To use open and fry to heat.

VII. MILK PRODUCTS

56. Cheese Sauce

Rotel tomatoes found in this book are the perfect ingredient to add to this sauce. Serve it with some tortilla chips created from the flour tortilla recipe in the bread section of this book.

 Easy  30-Minutes

Ingredients

10 pound can of cheese sauce
15 half pint jars

Note: This is not a USDA tested recipe.

Preparation

Ladle sauce into clean sanitized 1/2 pint jars. Wipe the rims. Apply lids and rings. Place in a cool water bath. Slowly heat the water bath canner so the cheese heats up with the water. Bring to a rolling boil and water bath for 20 minutes.

NOTES:

_____
_____
_____
_____
_____
_____
_____
_____
_____
_____
_____

57. Cream Cheese

This cheese found its origin in a New York dairy in 1873 and captured America's attention. Its inherent velvetiness launched a wave of cream cheese lovers around the globe.

 Easy

 45-Minutes

Ingredients

cream cheese

Note: This is not a USDA tested recipe.

Preparation

Cut the cream cheese into cubes. Place in clean sanitized half pint jars. Melt the cream cheese right in the jars in a pan of water. Add more cream cheese and repeat until you get to the desired headspace of about ½ inch. Wipe the rims. Apply lids and rings. Process in a boiling water bath by bringing slowly up to a boil. Process at a rolling boil for 20 minutes. We have canned milk since the invention of canning however it was untested as it was:

1. Common practice no reason to test
2. Is a government commodity if you buy low and can it well you get around the government price fixing
3. The dairy lobby doesn't want you to can milk yourself they lose money. (a can of evaporated milk sells for almost more than a gallon of fresh milk) Follow the money trail and understand.

untested is not the same As unsafe

As with all recipes use your judgment as to what you want to try and your comfort level with canning and your canning safety standards.

58. Crockpot Yogurt

The ease of a crockpot speaks for itself; however, weight loss, bone density wellness, and heart health are just a few perks. Enrich your life with this wholesome product loved by men, woman, and children.

 Easy

 6 Hours plus 8-12 hours

Ingredients

½ gallon of milk
1 cup of plain yogurt

Preparation

Turn crock pot down on low and pour in a ½ gallon of milk. Heat on low for 2½ hours. Turn crock pot off and unplug it. Cool milk in the crock with the lid on for 3 hours. After 3 hours, add 1 cup of starter. I use one cup of plain yogurt with active cultures from the store (or I save from the last batch of homemade.) Make sure it is at room temperature. Stir thoroughly putting the cover back on and wrap in a towel.
Let set 8-12 hours or overnight store in a quart canning jar in the refrigerator. Tastes best after it has completely cooled. Note: Each batch made with leftover homemade yogurt gets progressively more tart so you may want to start with a fresh starter after a few batches. Homemade yogurt keeps longer than store bought. Tip: Use homemade jam as the fruit flavoring in the yogurt.

NOTES:

_____

59. Milk

Dairy lovers enjoy the convenience of canned milk. Now you can explore the possibilities that this process allows.

 Easy

 1 Hour

Ingredients

milk

Preparation

I canned milk two years ago about 45 pints. I am still using them. The process I used is simple. Put milk in pints. Bring up to 5 pounds of pressure. Turn the canner off and let cool completely before opening. The usual pressure for my altitude is 10 pounds of pressure but milk is done at 5 pounds of pressure at my altitude. It is one of the few exceptions to the "10-pound rule." I only use this in cooking as the milk sugars caramelize and the flavor changes slightly to a sweeter product. The milk fats will separate so shake before opening. This caramelization makes it really good in hot cocoa.

NOTES:

_____
_____
_____
_____

60. Shepherd Maple Butter

Melty, maple goodness brings out the flavor of rolls, pull-apart bread, crepes, sweet potatoes, squash, or toasted pecans. Having this on hand allows you to experiment with its uses in your recipes.

 Easy

 30 Minutes

Ingredients

½ cup maple sugar
4 pounds fresh sweet butter, softened

Preparation

Whip in blender until mixed thoroughly. Chill. Serve on hot buttered rolls.

THE SHEPHERD MAPLE STORY

In 1880 both sides of my mother's family settled in Shepherd, Michigan. As prominent citizens, they chose to plant Maple trees. These trees bring an enormous surplus of nectar that fills the town still today. Annually the Shepherd celebrates this sappy waffle topping in just about everything you can imagine from maple sugar, cake, pie, ice cream, candy, pancakes and so much more. Since 1966 the town has celebrated this tradition, and people flock to the Village of Shepherd to taste its sweet bounty. There are tractor pulls, arts and crafts, 5K and 10K races along with Pancake Dinners. This recipe comes from this great, and thus it is appropriately named "Shepherd Maple Butter." The proceeds from this event goes to the children of Shepherd to pay for things they need in the community.

VIII. PASTA & NOODLES

61. Grandma's Noodles

I make these by feel and you will too once you work with these noodles a few times. A #1 family favorite recipe.

 Easy

 1 Hour prep plus 2 days drying time

Ingredients

flour
egg yolks (save the broken shell of one egg)
sea salt
heavy whipping cream
milk or water

Preparation

These can be made ahead and after curing you can freeze them to pull out and use the chicken meal starter. Make a well in the center of your flour. Add your egg yolks and beat them slowly adding in the flour. Add the cream and continue to mix well. Coat a flat surface like a kitchen table with flour and roll noodle dough to a ¼ or less thickness. Noodles will swell when cooking so don't make them too thick to start. Let dry for a couple of days if the room's humidity allows otherwise pack in freezer bags after they are dried and not so sticky. Use more flour to coat if they are still sticky in texture. Freeze. Pull out and cook as needed. These are also good fresh so make sure to make enough to make some right away too. Cook boil the noodles in the chicken meal starter or chicken broth (with a pinch of poultry seasoning) until noodles are done or about 20 minutes. This recipe was handed down to Grandma Curtiss from her Grandma Eliza Jane (Minich) Thomas who had deep Pennsylvania German roots. This is my comfort food. Tip: Save the egg whites for scrambled eggs or making meringue.

62. Macaroni and Tomatoes

My dad enjoyed this dish so much, and I know you will too. Enjoy the perfect simplicity of this combination.

 Easy

 30-Minutes

Ingredients

1 quart home canned stewed tomatoes
1 pint canned ground beef with onions
1 pound macaroni noodles
sea salt to taste
pepper to taste

Preparation

Prepare macaroni following package directions. Drain. Add can of tomatoes and can of beef. Add more tomato juice if you like it more like a soup. Heat to a boil for 10 minutes. If made with fresh ground meat fry with onions until done. Then add to the prepared tomato and macaroni mixture. My dad grew up during the Great Depression and this was his go-to meal. Often he said they were too poor for meat and just ate it without meat and then he would add a pat of butter for a flavor to his bowl. Many times we had this for our Sunday night supper when I was growing up. Serve piping hot with slices of buttered bread. This is one of those recipes that can be stretched to feed a large family rather frugally.

NOTES:

_____
_____
_____

The barn in this photo is located across the street from the house that I lived in when I was six years old. I have a grand memory of when it was a productive place and painted so brightly. A couple of years ago it was destroyed in a storm and had sat as pictured ever since... The photo was taken for this cookbook to show a bit my area. The very next day I drove past it, and it was completely torn down. The Amish had asked to take it down for the wood and that they did. You may notice the pile of wood being stacked up on the right side of the barn as they strive to take it apart. The memories that you make in life are all you really have in the still of the night. I know you will create memories that last a lifetime with your friends and family by canning together and consuming all the delightful food as you share it with those around you. God bless you all as you teach others to live a life that will prepare them for any storm.

63. Tortellini In Marinara Sauce

Tortellini is pasta that has made its way into the hearts of many but complimented with the right marinara sauce; this is one meal destined to warm many tummies.

 Easy    1 Hour

Ingredients

dried cheese tortellini
marinara sauce

Note: This is not a USDA tested recipe.

Preparation

In each pint jar add 1/2 cup of tortellini. Add ¼ cup water to each jar. Fill with marinara sauce to one inch headspace. Stir it to remove air bubbles with a bamboo skewer and pressure can for 20 minutes at 10 pounds of pressure. May need to adjust for higher altitudes.

NOTES:

_____
_____
_____
_____
_____
_____
_____
_____
_____
_____

IX. SALADS

64. Cucumber And Onion Salad

The sweetness of the onion in this salad brings out the flavor of the cucumbers. Such a lovely way to serve them.

 Easy

 2 Hours

Ingredients

Preparation

1 thinly sliced raw cucumber

1 small sweet yellow onion

sea salt

3 tablespoons of white sugar

Pour white vinegar over one thinly sliced raw cucumber and small sweet yellow onion. Add 1 cup water. Add a pinch of sea salt and stir in 3 tablespoons of white sugar. Wait 20 minutes. Serve as a fresh summer side. Cover and refrigerate. Keeps a very long time in the fridge. We kept a container of this going in the fridge all summer as a kid and it would be pulled out and served as a side at both lunch and dinner times.

NOTES:

_____
_____
_____
_____
_____
_____
_____

65. Slaw

There is an art to making slaw. I believe the perfect head of cabbage and this syrup is the key to making a genuinely tasty mixture that all will love.

 Easy　　　　 2 Hours

Ingredients

1 medium head of cabbage
1 large carrot
1 green pepper
1 small onion
1 teaspoon salt

SYRUP
1 1/2 cup vinegar
3/8 cup water
1 cup sugar
1 teaspoon celery seeds
1 teaspoon mustard seeds

Preparation

Shred together vegetables then add the salt. Let stand for 1 hour. Drain water from vegetables. Boil syrup ingredients together for 1 minute. Cool. Pack into pint jars. Process in a boiling water bath for 15 minutes (I use 20 for quarts.) If you don't want to can this you may put it into freezer containers instead and freeze it. Leftovers may also be frozen. This slaw may be drained before use and mayonnaise added or used as is.

NOTES:
_____
_____
_____
_____
_____
_____
_____

X. VEGGIES

66. Beans

Beans, beans are good for your heart, indeed! They lower cholesterol and in turn, reducing one's cardiac risk.

 Easy    2 Hours

Ingredients

½ cup dried beans

salt (½ teaspoon salt to pints or 1 teaspoon to quarts)

Preparation

No soak method for canning dried beans. After rinsing you add ½ cup dried beans to each pint jar or 1 cup to each desired quart. Note: This is a level measure, not a rounded scoop! Adding too many beans can lead to lid failures. Add ½ teaspoon salt to pints or 1 teaspoon to quarts. Leave salt out if beans are very old. Adding salt to old beans before they soften can lead to tough beans. Fill with water or broth to the 1-inch headspace. Apply lids and rings. Process pints 75 minutes at 10 pounds pressure (may need to adjust for higher altitude) or 90 minutes for quarts. Tip: Save the liquid from canned garbanzo beans to use as an egg substitute in baking. This is called Aquafaba.

NOTES:

_____

_____

_____

67. Bean Soup (Grandma's)

Once again a here is a favorite recipe passed down from Grandma. A cup of this soup has many qualities that help build healthy bodies. For decades this has been a hit in our family.

 Easy

 3 Hours

Ingredients

1 medium onion diced fine

1 clove garlic minced (optional)

1 ham bone with some meat on it

2 pounds white great northern beans, soaked

2 cups ham or chicken broth

1-2 bay leaves

Preparation

While soaking the beans, simmer the ham bone and broth with the bay leaf, garlic and onions. When the meat all falls off the bone remove the bone and bay leaves. Add the pre soaked beans. Cook until beans are soft. Salt and pepper to taste (will depend of the saltiness of the ham if you need any salt at all.) Serve with cornbread. This can be canned pints at 75 minutes or quarts at 90 minutes at 10 pounds of pressure. May need to adjust for your altitude.

NOTES:
_____
_____
_____
_____
_____
_____
_____

68. Cauliflower (Pickled)

Chocked full of vitamin C and potassium you can use this pickled delicacy with excellent results. It is a superb veggie choice that promotes kidney health by fighting off toxins with the help of its folate and high fiber content.

 Easy

 90-Minutes

Ingredients

2 uncooked beets
1-quart white vinegar
1-quart water
1 tablespoon celery seeds
1 tablespoon sea salt
12 cups cauliflower florets (1 medium head)

Preparation

Peel and chop the beets. Combine with the vinegar and water. Bring almost to a boil, then simmer for 5 minutes. Strain. Give the beet pulp to the chickens if you have some. Pack each of 3 clean, hot, quart jars with 1 teaspoon celery seeds, 1 teaspoon salt, and 4 cups cauliflower florets. Leave about 3/4 inch headspace. Fill each jar with the brine, leaving about 1/2 inch headspace. Put on lids and rings. Process in a boiling water bath for 10 minutes. Makes 3 quarts.

NOTES:

_____
_____
_____
_____
_____
_____
_____

69. Corn Casserole (Thanksgiving)

Creamy corn finds its way to the table in one form or another at Thanksgiving, and this is our classic dish that all who try it come back for seconds and thirds. Create a new traditional dish for your family and friends to share.

 Easy

 1 Hour

Ingredients

1 pint canned corn
1 cup heavy cream
3 tablespoons flour
1 teaspoon powdered mustard
3 pats of butter

Preparation

Mix the corn, cream, flour and mustard in a buttered casserole dish. Top with one sleeve of crushed ritz crackers. Top with the cut up pats of butter. Bake at 350 degrees oven until golden brown about 30 minutes.

NOTES:

_____
_____
_____
_____
_____
_____
_____
_____
_____
_____
_____

70. Giardiniera (Overnight, Refrigerated)

Your choice of veggies dictation your unique version of this recipe. Slicing them thin allows the sweet and tanginess to come through.

 Easy

 1 Hour plus overnight

Ingredients

fresh vegetables thinly sliced
can of pickle brine
water or vinegar

Preparation

You can also make quick refrigerator pickles by canning your leftover pickle brine alongside the pickles for the same time as the recipe calls for the pickles. Later, when you have an abundance of fresh vegetables thinly slice them. Open a can of pickle brine and pour enough over the veggies to cover the veggies. If you don't have enough liquid to completely cover the fresh veggies you can add a small amount of water or vinegar. Let sit at least overnight to marinate in the refrigerator. Serve as a quick summer side. Tip: A mandolin cutter is great for thinly slicing veggies it is also great for slicing fingers so exercise caution. I recommend cut resistant safety gloves. Even the most seasoned canners have a love-hate relationship with the mandolin cutter. Beware!

71. Peppers In A Jar

Stuffed peppers find their origin in Spain and are very popular in the Basque region of the country. These are our American version with rice added along with the taco seasoning found in this cookbook to add just the right spices.

 Easy

 3 Hours

Ingredients

8 green bell peppers
2 pounds ground beef
2 cups long grain rice, uncooked
2 packages taco seasoning or equivalent home blend taco seasoning
2 pounds tomatoes

Preparation

Cut top off of 8 bell peppers that will fit through the wide mouth opening. Combine the raw meat, rice, taco seasoning, diced tomatoes. Fill peppers with the stuffing. Slide jars down over stuffed peppers so they will be upside down when you put on the lid. Pressure can for 75 minutes pressure for 10 pounds pressure or adjust for your altitude. They will come out of the jar right side up when you turn the jar over to slide them out then you turn the jar over to slide them out.

NOTES:

_____
_____
_____
_____
_____
_____
_____

72. Ranch Kale Chips

Kale is the "New Beef "and is higher in iron than beef. It has more calcium per calorie than dairy. Creating chips from Kale is a great way to consume this veggie, and the ranch dressing leaves you saying "I can eat just one."

 Easy

 3 Hours and 30 minutes

Ingredients

kale leaves
powdered ranch dressing
Olive Oil
sea salt

Preparation

Sprinkle Kale leaves with olive oil, sea salt, and ranch seasoning. Put in 170 degrees oven for about 3 hours. Turn the oven off and let it sit in the unopened oven till the oven until oven is cool. Makes very crispy chips.

NOTES:

_____
_____
_____
_____
_____
_____
_____
_____
_____
_____

73. Tomatoes (Green For Frying)

Using all one's tomato crop before they perish can present a challenge. Frying green tomatoes is simplified by opening a jar and use them as needed. Take time to preserve yours and put them on the table with ease.

 Easy

 90-Minutes

Ingredients

green tomatoes
sea salt
lemon juice

Preparation

I slice the green tomatoes about 3/8'-1/2 inch thick for canning. Pack green tomato slices in wide mouth jars with 1/2 teaspoon sea salt for pints and 1 teaspoon sea salt for quarts. Add 1/4 teaspoon lemon juice for pints an 1/2 teaspoon lemon juice to each quart. Fill the jars with water, leaving a 1/2 inch of headspace. Process pints for 7 minutes at 5 pounds of pressure. Quarts for 10 minutes at 5 pounds of pressure. You can water bath for 20 minutes but let them stay in the boiling water bath until it has cooled down some.

NOTES:

_____
_____
_____
_____
_____
_____

74. Tomatoes (Rotel)

Rotel tomatoes are the special ingredient in the chili con queso dip (Rotel) we all love with our tortilla chips. They are also tremendous added to many dishes, sauces, soups, casseroles and recipes. The sky's the limit.

 Easy

 3 Hours

Ingredients

ROTEL

4 quarts tomatoes, peeled and diced (about 12 pounds whole)

2 large bell peppers, diced

1 large onion, diced

4-8 seeded jalapeño peppers, chopped fine

Preparation

ROTEL

Mix all the vegetables together in a large pot. Add 3/4 cup apple cider vinegar and 1/4 cup sugar to the pot. Bring to a fun rolling boil then turn down the heat by adding 1/2 teaspoon of salt and 1 teaspoon of lemon juice in each. Fill jars with tomato mixture leaving headspace. Apply lids and rings. Process for 20 minutes in a water bath.

NOTES:

75. Tomatoes (Stewed)

The "Macaroni and Tomatoes" recipe found in the pasta section of this book gets its yumminess from these stewed tomatoes. Where will you use them?

 Easy

 90-Minutes

Ingredients

1-bushel tomatoes, meatier varieties work best I prefer Beefsteak tomatoes

sea salt

Note: This is not an USDA approved recipe because I do not add citric acid or lemon juice. To make this an approved recipe you would need to add ½ teaspoon citric acid or 2 tablespoon bottled lemon juice to each quart or add ¼ teaspoon citric acid or 1 tablespoon bottled lemon juice to each hot pint jar before processing.

Preparation

Wash tomatoes cut out any bad spots. Discard any spoiled or overly ripe tomatoes (overripe are best dehydrated rather than canned.) Blanch until skins wrinkle a few tomatoes at a time. Peel and core. Cut into quarters. Place in a large pan on the stove. Bring slowly to a gentle rolling boil. Pack into prepared jars and add ½ teaspoon of salt to each quart or ¼ to each pint. Pack tight, leaving one-inch headspace. Wipe the rims. Apply lids and rings. Process in a boiling water bath for 40 minutes for pints and 45 minutes for quarts, adjusting for altitude.

NOTES:

_____
_____
_____
_____
_____

NOTES:

Troubleshoot

1. Jar Rim

First thing is the rim of the jar ok. Look and feel sometimes you can't see the small imperfection but can feel it.

This is almost always the cause.

2. Check the recipe again

Was I tired and I missed a step? Failed to follow the recipe?

If I made up my own recipe did I use the times needed and method preferred?

3. Double check the times.

If I didn't follow the standard time then I should expect issues.

Know your times. This is one area even rebels need to be sure they are watching and staying in the zone.

4. Cleanliness.

I go above and beyond. Most of us do. Before I blame the lid I also review my procedure. But maybe we also have fermentation going on in the same kitchen area? If you are then you may have some cross contamination. That Scooby may be the culprit. Or maybe it is the sourdough.

These are innocent mistakes but NOT the fault of the lid manufacturer.

5. Lids

Check before you use them for poor gaskets on the lids.

Uneven, thin or narrow spots in the gasket will not seal.

6. Headspace.

Is it a headspace issue? Did you start out with enough headspace?

7. Quality of produce.

I saved the second most common reason for last. I am often given products that are just past prime. Yes, I can try can it to save it. But I also realize I will have more jar spoilage failures because of it. This is also not a lid issue but a quality control issue. The older the product means that the chemical compounds contained inside are breaking down causing gases some of these will not break down with heat after a certain period of time has passed. So the product can create more gases causing it to come unsealed. It might be better to dehydrate those way overripe tomatoes than to toss them in my sauce and can. It is easy to blame our failures on someone else but in all honesty, they are learning tools. We learn much more from failure than success. There is no shame in using them to step up.

NOTES:

Yields

A pound (454 grams) equals 2 cups or 280 ml weights and volumetric

6-8 Tablespoons pectin equals on a box of powdered pectin

Apples – 1 bushel – 40 to 50 pounds – 20 to 22-quart jars

Apricots – 1 bushel – 40 to 50 pounds – 20 to 24-quart jars

Blackberries – 1 bushel – 40 to 50 pounds – 22 to 24-quart jars

Cherries – 1 bushel – 40 to 50 pounds – 18 to 24-quart jars

Peaches – 1 bushel – 40 to 50 pounds – 18 to 24-quart jars

Pears – 1 bushel – 50 to 55 pounds – 25 to 28-quart jars

Pineapple – 1 crate – (no weight is given) – 12 to 16-quart jars

Plums – 1 bushel – 50 to 55 pounds – 24 to 26-quart jars

Beans Green – 1 bushel – 28 to 30 pounds – 15 to 18-quart jars

Beans, Dried-1/2 cup (6-8 oz) per quart or 1/4 cup (2-4 ounces) per pint jar

Beets – 1 bushel – 50 to 60 pounds – 18 to 22-quart jars

Carrots – 1 bushel – 50 to 60 pounds 18 to 22-quart jars

Corn – 1 bushel – 60 to 70 pounds – 8 to 12-quart jars

Greens – 1 bushel – 12 to 14 pounds – 6 to 8-quart jars

Peas (In Pod) – 1 bushel – 28 to 30 pounds – 6 to 8-quart jars

Pumpkin-1 1/2 pounds with the raw skin on yields 2 cups mashed cooked

Tomatoes (whole) – 1 bushel – 50 to 60 pounds – 14 to 20-quart jars

"A Pint is a pound the world around"-author unknown

How man apples do i buy to make a pie? Or 15 pies?

1 Pound of Apples = 3 medium apples = 2 cups sliced

3 Pounds of Apples = 8 to 9 medium apples = one 9 inch pie

1 Peck of Apples = 10 to 12 pounds = 32 medium apples = three to four 9-inch pies = 7 to 9 quarts frozen apples = 4 quarts canned

1 bushel of apples = 48 pounds = 126 medium apples = fifteen 9-inch pies = 30 to 36 pints frozen = 16 to 19 quarts canned

Which kinds of apples make the best pie?

The answer to this is the individual which makes it complicated. First, to answer it I need to know what kind of pie do you like? Describe the texture, is it sweet or tart?, Is it full of firm apple slices or runny? Mom made her apple pie with MacIntosh apples. I would describe it as the middle of my scale. But to make a firmer pie use, I use a firmer apple, something like a granny smith. Now for a juicy and more sauce-like pie use one of the softer sweeter apples like a Golden Delicious. For me at least the answer is to use a mix of apples, so I have some firm slices and some sweet juiciness. Buying a blend of apples makes my pie layered in apple flavor and texture.

Measurement	Equivalent
3 teaspoons	1 tablespoon
4 tablespoons	1/4 cup
5-1/3 tablespoons	1/3 cup
10-2/3 tablespoons	2/3 cup
12 tablespoons	3/4 cup
16 tablespoons	1 cup
1 tablespoons	1/2 fluid ounce
1 cup	1/2 pint
2 cups	1 pint
4 cups	1 quart
2 pints	1 quart
4 quarts	1 gallon

Canning Methods

Open Kettle is the oldest of all canning methods and no longer recognized by the USDA. Used primarily for high acid foods like tomatoes and applesauce or pear sauce. Critical step: Sanitize your jars and lids and utensils before filling. Leave a half inch headspace. Drawbacks: It is not suitable for long-term storage. It was only intended to keep people fed for six months of winter until the next growing season.

Steam canning method

This method goes in and out of favor. Currently, it is again approved. It is similar to water bath canning but requires a particular canner. It also uses less water. Also, need to sanitize the jars before filling. Do not allow jars to touch. You can use your pressure canner as a steam canner.

Water Bath Method

Approved Use for fruits and high acid foods like pickles. The Amish and Rebels and many people other worldwide also use this for low acid foods. Doing so requires a lengthy time. Minimal equipment is needed. Large stock pot with a cover is good enough if you can keep jars covered by 2 inches with boiling water. Also, need to sanitize the jars before filling.

Critical Step is not to start timing until water is at a full rolling boil and to keep the extra water boiling handy to keep up the level.

Pressure cooker method

Used for low acid foods and high acid. This method requires a pressure canner. Good for long-term storage.

It is quicker than a water bath.

Sanitizing jars

Wash in hot soapy water. And then rinse. Bring to boil for 10 Minutes. Higher elevations than 1,000 feet above sea level require another minute for every 1,000 feet in elevation.

About The Author And Editor

Tammy McNeill, the Author, is a Michigan native and currently lives there with her family. Tammy has raised natural children, adopted children, stepchildren and has fostered children. Tammy's oldest daughter Jessica is a lawyer while one of her other daughters is a very active mom. Tammy's, son Taylor, is very talented and owns his own construction business. Her daughter Camryn is a college student. Currently at home is Lizzi, her 15-year-old, a freshman in high school, Jon who is a 13-year-old middle school student and last but not least her son, Sawyer who is 10 and in third grade. As a grandmother to 5 grandchildren, she is truly blessed and strives to pass her knowledge to them as well. Tammy's parents instilled a belief system in Tammy that still guides her. Her faith gives her courage, patience, wisdom and the freedom to be herself and to teach others her passion. Tammy's family has always been the focus of her life and showing those around her how to make and put up their own food is a top priority for her. The practice of self-sustainable living is essential to her and wishes that everyone would try to preserve their food at least once.

Sheri Savory, the Editor, is a well-known cookbook and genetic genealogy book author. She is a Genetic Genealogist, Mother, Grandma, and Baker. Sheri currently lives in Los Angeles, CA with her daughter and two granddaughters. Sheri and Tammy both share the McNeil (Sheri) McNeill (Tammy) last name. Sheri has a great-grandfather born in Alvinston, ON. Tammy's grandfather McNeill was also born in the small Canadian town. Recently they made acquaintances when Tammy contacted Sheri to try to find their genealogical connection. Unable to verify their McNeil/McNeill connection by DNA since their relationship is no doubt beyond the scope of the test available to them they continue to research the possibilities. Sheri published a cookbook from her mothers family recipes in 2018 called

Savory's Southern Specialties. In discussion with Tammy, she mentioned her desire to produce a cookbook for her Facebook group about canning. Sheri offered to help edit and design it which began the process. During the layout process of this book of Tammy and Sheri proved by luck that they indeed are cousins but NOT as McNeil/McNeill's, yet. Together they found traits and things in common that give them a greater understanding of each other.

For more information please contact Tammy McNeill at rebelcanners@gmail.com, http://www.starspublishing.com or https://www.facebook.com/groups/291961427669718/

Love "Southern cookbooks?" Tammy recommends this cookbook, Savory's Southern Specialties by, Sheri Savory.

Index

Symbols

10-pound rule 128
60 AD 102
1966 129

A

Abraham Lincoln 103
active cultures 125
allspice 23, 73
American 95, 117, 152
apple cider 22, 73, 82, 157
apples 27, 60, 73, 86
applesauce 12, 38, 73
Aquafaba 141
Army surgeon 102
Aunt Harriet 83

B

bacon 35
baking powder 52, 64, 99
Baklava 42
bamboo skewer 136
Basque region 152
baste 109
bay leaves 104, 144
beans 19, 34, 52, 141, 144
bean sprouts 117
beef 98, 103, 104, 133, 152, 153
beef bones 98
Beefsteak tomatoes 160
beets 145
black bean 19
black cherries 81
bone 98
Bourbon Whiskey 34
bread 51, 60, 68, 73, 76, 108, 109, 120, 121, 129, 133
bread slices 108
brine 22, 104, 145, 149
broth 98, 102
brown sugar 18
Bundt pan 57
butter 12, 18, 35, 38, 50, 57, 61, 64, 73, 76, 81, 83, 129, 133, 148
buttered bread 133

C

cabbage 140
cake 57
canned corn 148
canned water 98
canning 5, 13, 30, 35, 39, 80, 86, 90, 98, 104, 125, 134, 141, 149, 156
canning addiction 98
caramelization 128

caramelize 128
carcasses 98
carrot 64, 98, 102, 140
carrot peels 98, 102
casserole 50, 148
casserole dish 50, 148
cauliflower 145
cauliflower florets 145
cayenne 22, 23
cayenne pepper 22, 23
celery seed 16, 22, 43, 46
celery seeds 13, 140, 145
cheddar 105
cheesecloth 30, 90
cheese sauce 121
cheese tortellini 136
cherry 81
chicken 22, 98, 99, 102, 116, 132, 144
chicken meal starter 132
chocolate chips 53, 64
Christmas 53, 56, 61, 64, 105
cinnamon 12, 23, 51, 64, 72, 73, 76
citric acid 160
Clear Jel 39
Clingstone 80
clover blossoms 30
cloves 16, 23, 64, 76, 98, 102, 104, 117

cooked rice 116
cookies 61, 64, 77
cookie trays 61
Cool Whip 57
copyright 2
cornbread 144
corn casserole 148
Corned Beef 103
Corned Venison 104
cough suppressant 94
cousin Ray 117
crackers 22, 105, 108, 148
cranberries 23, 27
cranberry 23, 27, 65
cream cheese 22, 105, 124
crockpot 73, 125
cucumbers 16, 43, 46, 137
curing 132

D

deep frying 117
degrees 50, 57, 61, 64, 69, 109, 148, 153
dehydrate 91
dehydrated lemon zest 81
De Materia Medica 102
deviled 108
dried beans 141

E

edible flowers 94

egg roll 116, 117
egg roll wrappers 117
egg substitute 141
egg yolks 132
elderberry bushes 83
elderberry juice 83
Emperor Nemo 102
Equivalent 168
extract 34

F

Facebook 5
Fiddleheads 13
Fireweed 30
flour 19, 38, 52, 61, 64, 99, 120, 121, 132, 148
flour tortilla 19, 120, 121
Foley food mill 12
freeze 51, 64, 76, 94, 104, 117, 132, 140
French 9, 51
fruit flavoring 125
fruit leather 72
fry 51, 117, 120, 133
Frying 156

G

garbanzo beans 141
garlic 16, 22, 98, 102, 104, 117, 120, 144
garlic powder 22, 120

gelatin 56
Giardiniera 149
ginger 76, 116, 117
glaze 57, 109
golden delicious apples 27
Grandma 83, 132, 144
Grandma Curtiss 132
Grandma Eliza Jane (Minich) 132
Granny Smith 73
granulated sugar 82
greased 57, 64
Great Depression 133
green chili 19
green onions 105, 117
green peppers 16, 112, 116
green tomatoes 156
ground beef 133, 152
ground ham 109

H

ham 82, 105, 108, 109, 112, 144
ham and cheese 105
ham bone 144
hamburger 117
headspace 13, 22, 35, 39, 60, 65, 68, 82, 86, 103, 108, 112, 113, 116, 120, 124, 136, 141, 145, 157, 160
heavy cream 148

heavy whipping cream 132
higher altitudes 19, 35, 65, 98, 104, 120, 136
high fiber 145
homemade bread 108
hot cocoa 128
hot dogs 95
hot pack 27, 68

I

ice cream 39, 60, 73, 77, 81, 129
Inaugural Dinner 103
Influenza 90
ingredients 12, 13, 16, 18, 19, 22, 23, 27, 30, 34, 35, 38, 39, 42, 43, 46, 50, 51, 52, 53, 56, 57, 60, 61, 64, 65, 68, 69, 72, 73, 76, 77, 80, 81, 82, 83, 86, 87, 90, 91, 94, 95, 98, 99, 102, 103, 104, 105, 108, 109, 112, 113, 116, 117, 120, 121, 124, 125, 128, 129, 132, 133, 136, 137, 140, 141, 144, 145, 148, 149, 152, 153, 156, 157, 160
instant chocolate pudding 53

J

jalapeños 22
jam 27, 39, 61, 77, 80, 81, 125
jars 12, 13, 16, 22, 23, 27, 30, 35, 39, 42, 46, 60, 68, 76, 77, 80, 81, 82, 83, 86, 87, 94, 95, 98, 102, 103, 108, 116, 120, 121, 124, 140, 145, 152, 156, 157, 160
Jell-O 56
jelly 23, 30, 42, 80, 82, 83, 86, 87, 91, 94, 108, 112
jelly sandwiches 83
Juice 86, 90

K

Kale 153
Kale Chips 153
Karen Stearns 9
ketchup 116
kidney 145
kosher salt 104

L

Ladle 30, 35, 39, 42, 60, 76, 121
Lard 35
lard sandwiches 83
Laura's egg rolls 116
lemon 34
lemon juice 12, 42, 56, 77, 83, 86, 156, 157, 160
lettuce 108
lids 13, 19, 35, 60, 65, 68, 77, 80, 81, 83, 86, 95, 103, 113,

120, 121, 124, 141, 145, 157, 160
long grain rice 152

M

macaroni noodles 133
mace 73
Macintosh 73
mandolin cutter 149
maple sugar 129
maple syrup 18, 51
marinade 22
marinara sauce 136
mayonnaise 108, 140
measurement 168
meatier sauce 73
meringue 132
Michigan 5
milk 35, 46, 50, 51, 99, 105, 109, 125, 128, 132
milk sugars 128
mini chocolate chips 53
mini marshmallows 53
mint 34
molasses 60, 76
mother 12, 38, 83, 117, 129
mustard 13, 16, 22, 46, 104, 108, 109, 140, 148
mustard seed 16, 22, 46, 104

N

New York 124
nonfat dry milk 46
noodles 132
notes 13, 16, 17, 23, 26, 27, 30, 31, 38, 39, 42, 43, 46, 47, 50, 51, 52, 53, 56, 57, 61, 64, 72, 76, 77, 81, 82, 86, 87, 95, 102, 103, 104, 105, 108, 109, 112, 113, 116, 117, 121, 125, 128, 133, 136, 137, 140, 141, 144, 145, 148, 152, 153, 156, 157, 160, 161, 165
nutmeg 76
nuts 64

O

oil 38, 57, 69, 117, 153
omelette 112
orange 27, 34, 60, 65
orchard 73
Oreo 53
overnight 42, 46, 87, 149

P

pancake mix 50
pan greasing 38
pasta 132
peach 80
Peach Schnapps 80
pears 12
pear sauce 12

pecans 57, 129
pectin 77, 80, 81, 82, 83, 86, 87, 94
Pedacius Dioscorides 102
Pennsylvania German 132
pepper 22, 23, 95, 99, 112, 113, 120, 140, 144
peppers 16, 22, 46, 112, 116, 152, 157
pickle 13, 16, 149
pies 60, 68, 73
Pin 81
pineapple 39
pineapple chunks 116
pineapple juice 109, 116
plant 129
pork 22, 82, 109, 113, 117
pork chops 82
pork sausage 117
potassium 145
potatoes 103, 113, 129
potato masher 90, 91
potato peels 98
pounds of pressure 19, 35, 68, 95, 98, 104, 108, 113, 116, 120, 128, 136, 144, 156
powdered fruit pectin 82
powdered mustard 148
powdered sugar 51, 94
preparation 12, 13, 16, 18, 19, 22, 23, 27, 30, 34, 35, 38, 39, 42, 43, 46, 50, 51, 52, 53, 56, 57, 60, 61, 64, 65, 68, 69, 72, 73, 76, 77, 80, 81, 82, 83, 86, 87, 90, 91, 94, 95, 98, 99, 102, 103, 104, 105, 108, 109, 112, 113, 116, 117, 120, 121, 124, 125, 128, 129, 132, 133, 136, 137, 140, 141, 144, 145, 148, 149, 152, 153, 156, 157, 160
pulp 68, 145
pumpkin 68, 69, 76
pumpkin butters 76
pumpkin puree 76
pumpkin seeds 69

R

Rabbit 98
raisins 64
ranch dressing 153
rebelcanners 9
Red Haven peaches 80
red hots heart candy 82
red peppers 22, 46
red potatoes 113
refrigerate 53, 76, 90
relish 27, 46
rhubarb 60, 72
rings 13, 19, 35, 65, 68, 77, 80,

81, 83, 86, 95, 103, 113, 120, 124, 141, 145, 157, 160
ritz crackers 148
rolled oats 109
rose petals 42
Rotel tomatoes 121, 157
rotisserie chicken 98
Rum 57

S

salads 137
Schnapps 80
scrambled eggs 132
sea salt 16, 43, 99, 120, 145, 153, 156
seasoning 120
self-sufficient 5
self-sustained 9, 83
serve 19, 50, 51, 113, 116, 137
Shephard 129
shortening 35, 52, 64
slaw 140
slice of bread 51
soup 102, 144
soy sauce 116, 117
Spain 152
spices 16, 22, 51, 73, 82, 117, 152
Splenda 90, 91
squash 76, 129
starter 99, 125, 132
sterilized 94
stewed tomatoes 160
stock pot 98
St Patrick's Day 103
strawberries 60, 77
sugar 13, 16, 18, 22, 23, 27, 30, 39, 42, 43, 46, 51, 57, 60, 61, 64, 65, 72, 73, 76, 77, 80, 81, 82, 83, 86, 87, 90, 91, 94, 99, 104, 109, 116, 129, 137, 140, 157
sugar factory 83
sugar-free 90, 91
Sunday night 133
Sure Gel 91
sweet and sour 116
sweet butter 129
sweet relish 46
sweet yellow onion 137

T

Tabasco 95
taco 52, 120, 152
taco meat 120
taco seasoning 120, 152
Taiwanese 117
Tammy McNeill 2
tarter juice 65
tea 30, 42, 87, 94

teaching 5
Thanksgiving 61, 148
thumbprint 61
Tip 38, 46, 51, 60, 64, 65, 76, 91, 94, 99, 125, 132, 141, 149
tomato juice 133
topping 39
tortellini 136
tortilla chips 121, 157
toxins 145
troubleshoot 164
turkey 98, 102
turmeric 13, 16, 22

U

USDA 5, 35, 76, 121, 124, 136

V

vanilla 18, 34, 50, 51
vanilla beans 34
vegetable oil 38, 117
vegetables 16, 52, 140, 149, 157
vegetable scraps 98
veggies 5, 64, 112, 149
Village of Shephard 129
vitamin C 145
Vodka 34

W

walnuts 57

white mini marshmallows 53
white sugar 22, 23, 42, 60, 76, 80, 137
white vinegar 13, 16, 23, 43, 46, 104, 116, 137, 145
whole black peppercorns 104
Wild Choke 81
wild game brisket 104
Wild Violet 94
Worcestershire sauce 105
WWII 83

Y

yellow cake mix 57
Yogurt 125

Z

zest 27, 34, 60, 65, 77, 81
zucchini 12, 64

NOTES:

www.ingramcontent.com/pod-product-compliance
Lightning Source LLC
Chambersburg PA
CBHW061225150426
42811CB00057BB/1322